DISRAELI

D0162057

PROFILES IN POWER
General Editor: Keith Robbins

. . . . .

DISRAELI

Ian Machin

LONGMAN
London and New York

Longman Group Limited,
Longman House, Burnt Mill,
Harlow, Essex CM20 2JE, England
and Associated Companies throughout the world.

Published in the United States of America
by Longman Publishing, New York

© Longman Group Limited 1995

All rights reserved, no part of this publication may be
reproduced, stored in a retrieval system, or transmitted
in any form or by any means, electronic, mechanical,
photocopying, recording, or otherwise without either the
prior written permission of the Publishers or a licence
permitting restricted copying in the United Kingdom issued
by the Copyright Licensing Agency Ltd.,
90 Tottenham Court Road, London W1P 9HE.

First published 1995

ISBN 0 582 09806 8 CSD
ISBN 0 582 09805 X PPR

British Library Cataloguing-in-Publication Data

A catalogue record for this book is
available from the British Library

Library of Congress Cataloging-in-Publication Data

Machin, G. I. T.
  Disraeli / G.I.T. Machin.
    p.   cm. — (Profiles in power).
  Includes bibliographical references and index.
  ISBN 0–582–09806–8 (csd). — ISBN 0–582–09805–X (ppr)
  1. Disraeli, Benjamin, Earl of Beaconsfield, 1804–1881. 2. Great Britain—
Politics and government—1837–1901. 3. Prime ministers—Great Britain—
Biography.   I. Title. II. Series: Profiles in power (London, England)
DA564.B3M27   1995
941.081'092—dc20
[B]
                                                          94–11277
                                                          CIP

Set by 5P in 10½ Baskerville Linotronic 202
Produced by Longman Singapore Publishers (Pte) Ltd
Printed in Singapore

CONTENTS

CONTENTS

ACKNOWLEDGEMENTS

This book rests on four supports. First I would like to thank Professor Chris Wrigley, Professor (now Principal) Keith Robbins, and Longman Group, who were associated with the antecedents of my being invited to write this book, or with the invitation itself. Longman staff were also very helpful in other ways regarding the writing of the book.

Secondly, this work has partly emerged from research I did for previous books on Disraeli's period. I am grateful to the custodians of the 'Hughenden Papers' (the main collection of Disraeli correspondence) – first the National Trust at Hughenden Manor, near High Wycombe, and then the Bodleian Library – for allowing me to see these papers.

Thirdly, I would like to thank students, seminar groups, and audiences at historical addresses, who have listened to and discussed various matters relating to Disraeli's career introduced by myself. These include many generations of undergraduates in the Victorian Studies class at Dundee University; some postgraduate researchers; practising members of the Historical Association branches at Bangor, Glasgow and Dundee; participants in a Historical Association Sixth Form Conference at Durham; and attenders at one of the Christmas Lectures at Dundee University. In particular, the Historical Association members in my seminar group on nineteenth-century British politics and society at the summer school held at St Andrews in 1993 helped, by their incisive and judicious discussion, to focus and refine my views on points and issues about to be committed to this book.

Finally, I have not formally dedicated this book to my wife and family, as they have received this tribute before. But the fact that acknowledgement to them is made less formally this time does not mean that I am any the less indebted to them in a whole variety of ways.

Ian Machin
Newport-on-Tay
February 1994

Chapter 1

INTRODUCTION: DISRAELI AND POWER

> Power! Oh! what sleepless nights, what days of hot anxiety! what exertions of mind and body! what travel! what hatred! what fierce encounters! what dangers of all possible kinds, would I not endure with a joyous spirit to gain it![1]

Thus spoke the hero of Disraeli's first published novel, *Vivian Grey*, a semi-autobiographical romance. It is abundantly clear that the search for power was not only Vivian Grey's but Disraeli's own compelling pursuit. He would not be content with an obscure or subordinate role, but was always trying to urge himself to the front. His most famous phrase, 'I have reached the top of the greasy pole', uttered when he became Prime Minister in 1868, was not merely a flippancy but a heartfelt expression of relief and satisfaction at having gained a position he had been aiming at for thirty years. When, on top of this, he gained in 1874 a majority in the House of Commons to give his power much more substance than in his first ministry, he was triumphant indeed. By then he had risen from what were, for his era and his country, unusual and unpromising origins, to become arguably the most powerful person in the world, the virtual ruler of its richest land and its largest empire.

In his early years it was not clear what main channel Disraeli's search for fame and fortune would eventually select, whether it would be journalism, the writing of novels and poetry, or politics. Before he was thirty, however, the main thrust of his ambition had become directed towards political achievement. This was a line of effort in which he would not have to resign himself to the possibility of

1

merely posthumous fame, but would have to gain eminence and adulation during his life if he was to gain them at all. The following passage occurs in another of his earlier novels, *Contarini Fleming*:

> What were all those great poets of whom we talk so much? What were they in their life-time? The most miserable of their species. Depressed, doubtful, obscure, or involved in petty quarrels and petty persecutions. ... A man of great energies aspires that they should be felt in his life-time, that his existence shall be rendered more intensely vital by the constant consciousness of his multiplied and multiplying power. Is posthumous fame a substitute for all this?[2]

Disraeli's struggle for power and his attainment of it have proved endlessly fascinating, not only on account of the colourful and romantic features which accompanied them, but because of the exceptionally long distance he had to rise in order to get where he did. He should not, however, be credited with spuriously humble or alien origins. Although he was only a second-generation D'Israeli to be born in Britain, his family was wealthy, relatively cultured and well educated, and firmly established in English commercial, professional and literary circles. But no other Briton in the nineteenth century had to rise so far in order to attain the premiership; no other reached that position, as he did, without having the conventional trappings of public-school and university education. Apart from the Duke of Wellington he was the only British premier of his century who did not attend a university. He was also the one with the least auspicious social background for such an office. The political world of his day was indeed changing under the impact of the Industrial Revolution and the sporadic clamour for democratisation. But in spite (or because) of the Reform Act of 1832, politics were still heavily dominated by the landed aristocracy when Disraeli entered Parliament in 1837; and in spite (or because) of Disraeli's Reform Act of 1867 they remained dominated by it, though less so, when he died in 1881. For a non-aristocrat to gain admission to this exclusive, tightly knit political world, still more to rise to dominate it, required the possession and application of great intelligence, skill, persistence, and driving power. It was no wonder that

Samuel Smiles, in his celebrated book on *Self-Help*, extolled Disraeli as a shining example of 'the power of industry and application in working out an eminent political career'.[3]

Disraeli's great rival Gladstone had a very rich and ambitious middle-class father, who became an MP when Gladstone was seven and who was thus already in the world of high politics when his son, the future premier, was growing up. Gladstone was educated at Eton and Christ Church, Oxford, and gained entry to Parliament virtually on the strength of a speech he had made in the Oxford Union which impressed a powerful Tory patron, the Duke of Newcastle. Gladstone, like Disraeli, sought to enter an aristocratic world from outside, but was more advantageously situated in trying to breach its walls. Non-aristocrats like Disraeli and Gladstone who wanted to get into Parliament had to rely on money, education, talent and patronage in order to do so. Gladstone benefited a great deal from all four of these. Disraeli owed a lot to talent and patronage, but less to money and a good deal less to education than his rival.

The fact that Disraeli was Jewish was probably less of a handicap to him than is often imagined. His baptism as a Christian in youth was indispensable to his political prospects, as entrance to the House of Commons was not permitted until 1858–60 to those who were Jewish in religion and consequently could not take the oath of Christian allegiance. But apart from his adherence to the Christian faith much about him remained Jewish, not least his lasting admiration of Judaism and the achievements of his race. A Christianised Jew was unlikely to meet any firm obstruction in trying to pursue a parliamentary career in a liberal age. Others, such as Ralph Bernal and David Ricardo, had followed the same road before him. That Disraeli was a Conservative would make him no more likely than a Liberal to be hampered on this account. Provided he showed due respect for the aristocratic leaders of his party – as Disraeli was abundantly willing to do – he would be welcomed in order to show how Conservatives were not to be outdone in liberal attitudes. Thus his rise to be a Conservative leader and premier received no obvious impediment from his racial origins.

His Jewishness no doubt added greatly to his sense of distinctiveness and his pride in achievement. But at the same time it made him determined to rid himself of any unduly alien strain, and to adopt as much of the attitudes and habits of an insider as was necessary to rise to the leadership of his country. He fully succeeded in this aim, but stayed sufficiently the outsider to remain unique. He was a Christian, but retained much respect for the Jewish faith and was not afraid to advertise this in Parliament even though it found no answering echo. He became a country gentleman, but in artificial and straitened circumstances. He was an intensely practical politician who remained a practising novelist. He knew the world intimately and lived very much in it – constantly attending dinner parties and making visits as a guest to country houses – but he was never entirely of it. He reserved a separate personal area of retreat, from which he contemplated in ironic literary detachment the doings and foibles of his fellows. He would describe his impressions in letters, novels, and private notes on personalities. As Lord Blake has said, Disraeli never became an insider but rather a ruler of insiders.[4]

Even when he occupied positions at the very centre of power he remained an outsider with a strong exotic touch. The sense of mystery which attended him, oddly combined with his willingness (especially as he grew older) to accept all conventional norms, added considerably to his effectiveness. He flattered his peers by emulating them, but at the same time excited widespread curiosity by his individuality. If Gladstone was 'the People's William', Dizzy was the people's Asian wonder.

Disraeli's notable capacity for calm, detached self-containment emphasised his personal contrast from the voluble, excitable Gladstone. This difference, which was shown repeatedly in their contrasting styles on the floor of the House of Commons, was well marked by Sir Frederick Ponsonby, son of Queen Victoria's private secretary. Ponsonby met both statesmen as a boy. Of the Liberal leader he gave the following picture:

> Once Gladstone at luncheon was indulging in a scathing attack on the rising generation, pouring scorn on their lack of all knowledge of the classics; and in order to illustrate his point and show the lamentable ignorance that now prevailed, he suddenly turned to me. . . . He asked me what the quantity was of some syllable in a quotation from Horace. I had never heard of the

quotation and had no idea whether it was long or short, but as I was clearly expected to say something I said 'long'. He thumped the table and cried triumphantly, 'That is what everyone says', and I felt like a man who has backed a winner by mistake. Then in his grand manner he continued, 'But that is wrong, quite wrong; it is short, not long . . .'

Ponsonby's impression of Disraeli was quite different:

I remember walking with my two brothers behind Lord Beaconsfield and my father to Whippingham Church [near Osborne]; my father was stopped by someone on the road for a few minutes, and we three boys walked on with the sphinx-like Prime Minister. He suddenly asked us where some island in the East was, and of course we didn't know. He murmured, 'My boys, you will probably never get on because you don't know where this island is, but no one expects the British Prime Minister to know where it is'. He then relapsed into silence until my father caught us up.[5]

The most consistent strand in Disraeli's career was his determination to gain and keep political power. There was no similar consistency in the principles or policies he adopted when he was striving to win power or to keep it. He was entirely pragmatic in the way he took up and discarded policies as seemed suitable to his salient quest. When it came to putting policies into effect, he much preferred to dazzle by triumphant strokes than to grind away at a cause through thick and thin. He would be at the centre of political action himself when a *coup* was being executed, but when the enactment of policy required calm, steady planning and humdrum deliberation he would sometimes (though not always) leave the practical work to others while patronising them with his support.

Of the four lines of policy with which Disraeli was chiefly concerned – economic, social, electoral and imperial – economic policy provides the clearest example of his variable approach. Against the interest of his party's unity and future strength, but in favour of his hopes of advancing to a leading position in the party, he championed Protection as a means of challenging and overthrowing Peel in 1846. In

1852, however, he effectively abandoned ideas of restoring Protection in order to aid his party's electoral fortunes; though he would doubtless have taken Protection up again later if this had seemed strongly desirable for the national economy or his party's prosperity.

Imperial consolidation and expansion concerned him little, except on rare occasions, until the 1870s. Indeed, as Chancellor of the Exchequer in 1852, hard-pressed to save money and meet expenses, he complained that 'the colonies are a millstone round our necks'; and in 1866, when he was Chancellor again, he described them as 'deadweights'. But in 1868, when he was Prime Minister, he welcomed the success of a military expedition to Abyssinia. A few years later, when imperial questions mainly concerned the East, his oriental interests were aroused. He was drawn to exploit the political and economic opportunities offered by the Suez Canal, opened in 1869. He agreed, though with reluctance, that Britain's overseas commitments might be supported by giving Queen Victoria the title of Empress of India; and with much more enthusiasm he acquired Cyprus as an Eastern Mediterranean base. He carried out imaginative and popular strokes of policy which acknowledged the current importance of Empire but did not represent any systematic, long-term plan of colonial expansion on his part or rule out possible moves towards devolution.

Electoral (or 'parliamentary' reform), on the other hand, occupied Disraeli in some form or another for a good deal of his political life. He welcomed the Reform Act of 1832, seeing it as an aid to his ambition to enter Parliament, and a few years later he showed some sympathy with the Chartists. In the later 1840s, trying to develop lines of policy which would increase support for his party, he began to advocate moderate parliamentary reform even before the Liberals revived the same object. He was instrumental in introducing the first Conservative Parliamentary Reform Bill in 1859 and passing the second in 1867. Thereafter he showed no concern to take the subject further because it did not seem to be in his party's interest to do so.

Social reform was, somewhat surprisingly, a less constant light on Disraeli's path than parliamentary reform. Whereas the latter was of fairly continuous interest to him as a policy from 1848 to 1868, he showed a less consistent attachment to social reform. The interest he showed in this in the earlier 1840s did not revive in any clear way until the mid-1860s. The leader of 'Young England' and the author of *Sybil* was of course genuinely concerned about improving the condition of the people. But he was quite lacking in the personal traits needed to become, like his fellow-Conservative Lord Shaftesbury, a continuous verbal and literary exponent of the virtue and necessity of social improvements. Shaftesbury was primarily a preacher and crusader, Disraeli primarily a politician and *littérateur*. As a politician, and especially one who aspired to lead, Disraeli had to tailor his reforming urge to the nature, composition and demands of his party. The Conservative party aimed to unify all classes, preserving aristocratic ascendancy as far as possible but meeting some of the demands and alleviating the grievances of the rising middle and working classes. The Liberals also tried to be a party of all classes, but their composition was more disparate, and aristocratic power was under much more pressure from below than it was among the Conservatives; consequently they were more liable to fracture. Disraeli had a realistic, and in some respects a humanitarian, appreciation of the need for reforms, but his attempts to put this into practice were tempered and limited by his party political position.

For Disraeli, then, social reforms like other policies were subordinated to political expediency. Consequently, his support for such reforms was sporadic and inconsistent. He favoured them in general so long as *laissez-faire* was not much infringed. He opposed the New Poor Law of 1834 as a backbencher in the late 1830s and early 1840s, but did not urge its repeal when in office because this was not wanted by his party. He opposed the Public Health Bill of 1848 on *laissez-faire* grounds, and in 1850 he resisted government inspection of coal-mines in order to please aristocratic friends who were mine-owners. It was only by the mid-1860s, and still more clearly by the 1870s when at last he had a majority, that he was able to combine personal interest with political expediency and encourage the passing of a valuable if limited collection of social measures.

In an unsystematic and incoherent way – one completely lacking in any ideological commitment and sometimes pursuing a different line altogether – Disraeli followed the general liberal course which British Governments adopted

7

in the 1820s and have maintained, more or less, until the present time. Moderate and piecemeal reform, he no doubt believed, was the right way to avoid any drift towards revolution and preserve much of the *status quo* – the monarchy, aristocratic ascendancy and Established Churches. Such reforming methods would increase the country's stability and prosperity by means of a judicious enlargement of electoral participation, a prudent widening of commercial opportunity, and social reforms of a kind which did not greatly transgress the conventions of *laissez-faire*. In spite of his rift from Peel in the 1840s, he basically agreed with Peel's pragmatic policy of reform. There came more to divide him over policy from Gladstone than from Peel, but even in regard to Gladstone the difference was not fundamental. Both Gladstone and Disraeli accepted a liberal and pragmatic approach to reform which was meant to preserve rather than destroy.

Disraeli was far too much of a realist to oppose practically all reform, as a few reactionary Conservatives would have preferred him to do; or, on the other hand, to emulate radical ideologues in pressing reform to extreme lengths, which would have driven him from his party leadership and ruined his career. No one was further from entertaining any general scheme of collectivism or socialism in order to transform society. He initiated a good deal of change, but did so strictly within the limits of party interest and the accepted conventions of his age. He was convinced that Conservatives should maintain this reforming attitude, especially in the position in which they found themselves after 1846, otherwise they might not survive as a party. This seemed to be the only approach which could gain power for his party and himself.

· · ·

NOTES

1. Quoted in R.W. Davis, *Disraeli*, London 1976, p. 15.
2. Quoted in E.T. Raymond, *Disraeli: the alien patriot*, London 1925, p. 17.
3. S. Smiles, *Self-Help*, centenary edition, London 1958, p. 54.
4. R. Blake, *Disraeli*, London 1966, p. 17.
5. Sir F. Ponsonby (first Lord Sisonby), *Recollections of Three Reigns*, ed. C. Welch, London 1951, pp. 3–4.

Chapter 2

STRUGGLE IN YOUTH, 1804–1837

. . .

ORIGINS, RELIGION AND EDUCATION

To say that Benjamin Disraeli was born on 21 December 1804 at 6, King's Road, Bedford Row, London, to a family of Italian Sephardi Jews suggests that he was an alien arriving in the heart of the British capital. But both his father's and his mother's family were well established in England. He was third-generation British on his father's side and fifth-generation on his mother's, and both families were prosperous and accomplished. Disraeli's romantic dreams easily conjured up an aristocratic ancestry, on which he insisted as a fact. The reality, however, was that he came from a monied section of the middle classes which he was supposed to despise – but, according to his speeches and some of his political and personal actions, assuredly did not. His paternal grandfather, Benjamin D'Israeli, was born at Cento near Ferrara, and arrived in England as a youth in 1748 to sell straw hats and other goods from Italy.[1] From this he turned to stockbroking, in which he prospered. On his death in 1816 he left the large sum of £35,000, an amount representing over two million pounds at present-day value. This could not compare with the many more millions (in today's terms) which Gladstone's father had amassed by that date, but was quite enough to ensure that the successful financier's descendants could live in ample comfort and style.

To the family wealth was added a certain literary fame. Disraeli's father, Isaac D'Israeli, achieved a reputation as a literary antiquarian, historian and writer on Judaism. His *Curiosities of Literature* was widely read. He held liberal Tory views and had political acquaintances. Through him the young Benjamin met Canning and other Tory politicians.

9

But Isaac had no political ambitions himself, and, unlike Gladstone's father, did not plan a political career for his son. Benjamin seems to have decided on this most obvious route to power for himself.

The somewhat reclusive Isaac did not choose for his eldest son, Benjamin, the kind of education which indicated great ambition for his future, or even one which demonstrated and asserted his family's social position. The boy proceeded from a dame school to another school in London run by a Dissenting minister, Mr Potticary. Moreover, after Isaac had run into a personal quarrel with his synagogue and severed his relations with it, it was only with difficulty that a friend persuaded him to have his children baptised in the Christian faith. This step was then essential to any hope of a political career which Benjamin might have developed; but there is no evidence that such a hope on Benjamin's behalf entered Isaac's head. Isaac's younger children, Ralph and James, were baptised in the Church of England on 11 July 1817, at St Andrew's, Holborn. The two older children were christened later at the same church, Benjamin on 31 July and Sarah (who was two years senior to Benjamin) a month afterwards. This delay might suggest some resistance by Sarah and Benjamin, who were old enough to have personal views on the serious matter in hand.

Disraeli retained his allegiance to Christianity for the rest of his life, though in a rather individual fashion. He was knowledgeable about his religion, but perhaps rather superficially attached to it in some respects. He occasionally toyed with scepticism. His friend Lord Stanley referred in his diary to Disraeli's 'open ridicule, in private, of all religions', and to his having expressed the thought that 'the sentiment, or instinct, of religion would by degrees, though slowly, vanish as knowledge became more widely spread'. But Stanley ('Young Morose' to his peers) was very serious-minded, and such expressions probably indicated mere Disraelian speculation rather than firm views. Stanley did add: 'Disraeli is no materialist: he has always avowed his expectation of some form of future existence'.[2]

Disraeli certainly kept a strong regard for the faith he had left. His statement that 'I am the blank page between the Old Testament and the New' was not an admission of vacuity but a claim to be a reconciler of Judaism and Christianity.

However, since all he could suggest in this direction was that Jews should 'seek completion' by accepting Christ, he was unlikely to persuade many of his Hebrew brethren to adopt his unifying opinions. But the special significance of Judaism as the seed-bed of Christianity, sometimes urged with passionate rhetoric, was undoubtedly his chief religious concern.[3] Through this interest, as in his fascination with the Orient and with Jewish history, he retained a marked Jewish identity which accompanied, in characteristically individual form, his Christian faith.[4]

He knew a great deal about the diverse Christian doctrines and liturgical practices of his time, as is shown in his novel *Lothair*. But he observed them with a detached novelist's and politician's eye, and was not personally involved with the intense theological divisions of the Church of England or its differences from Nonconformists and Roman Catholics. In private he was apt to scorn Church disputes as nonsense.[5] But impartiality in such matters was reluctantly abandoned when he believed there was political advantage to be gained. On such occasions he entered ecclesiastical disputes in clear partisan fashion, even giving the impression that he was a leader in the fray.

After becoming a Christian, Disraeli was not sent to one of the famous Anglican public schools which might have seemed the natural destination for one of his social rank, particularly when his younger brothers were afterwards despatched to Winchester College. He was sent instead to a more obscure boarding establishment, Higham Hall in Essex, which was run by a Unitarian, the Rev Dr Eli Cogan. The fact that the school was for boarders casts doubt on the usual explanation that Disraeli was not sent to a famous boarding school because his mother was fearful of the rough behaviour at such places. The reason was probably that Isaac, who seems never to have accepted Christianity, sympathised with Unitarianism and knew Cogan as a sound classicist and a bibliophile. The high standard of education for which Dissenting establishments were known might have assisted the decision.

However, Benjamin was apparently not very happy or very successful at Higham Hall. He stayed there for less than three years and did not proceed to university. He left early in 1820, aged only fifteen. The remainder of his education was

11

obtained partly from his father and from a private tutor, but largely from reading in Isaac's vast library. This process of isolated learning no doubt added greatly to the exceptionally strong self-motivation possessed by 'a youth of immense ambition, consumed with an almost insolent determination to make his mark'.[6] The eventually spectacular results of his self-teaching made him well worth his honourable mention in *Self-Help*.

. . .

EARLY STRUGGLES: DEBTS AND WRITING

As yet, however, this compelling ambition lacked direction. In November 1821 Disraeli was articled to a firm of City solicitors in the Old Jewry. He later claimed that he was utterly unfitted to become a solicitor, and he did abandon his articles in 1825. But he did not give up all thought of a career in the law for several years. He contemplated becoming a barrister, enrolling at Lincoln's Inn in 1824 and keeping nine terms there, not removing his name until 1831. By 1823 he was writing a novel. But he could not be content with the uncertain prospect of gaining a fortune with his pen, and tried more direct methods of getting rich.

With some similarly adventurous friends he speculated in South American shares in the boom following the recognition of the newly independent states in that continent. But the boom burst, and by June 1825 the partnership had lost £7,000, some four hundred thousand pounds in today's terms. This was the beginning of massive indebtedness which afflicted Disraeli for four decades. He did not finally pay off his part of the 1825 debt until 1849. In the meantime he had incurred other large owings, and continued to do so in the 1850s. He was only freed from all of them by fortuitous circumstances in the early 1860s.

Benjamin had been further exercising his pen by writing pamphlets in defence of dubious and shaky South American mining companies. These pamphlets were published by John Murray (a friend of his father) for whom he was acting as a reader and assistant. His youthful tendency to court disaster continued. He was lured by the thought of fame through journalism to act with Murray and John Gibson Lockhart, son-in-law of Sir Walter Scott, in launching a new Conservative newspaper. Murray wrote to Lockhart about him in September 1825, in terms which he must later have greatly regretted: 'I never met with a young man of greater promise, from the sterling qualifications which he already possesses. He is a good scholar, hard student, a deep thinker of great energy, equal perseverance, and indefatigable application, and a complete man of business.'[7] The new paper was entitled *The Representative* by this precocious paragon. It was intended as a daily partner of Murray's successful *Quarterly Review*. But Dizzy lost more money in December 1825, when there was financial panic in London, and his gathering losses prevented him from stumping up his agreed portion of the capital to support *The Representative*. Consequently he abandoned his part in the venture before the paper collapsed after a run of only six months. The loss to Murray from this journalistic shipwreck was a huge £26,000.[8] If there was any positive result for Disraeli (which is doubtful), it was to strengthen his already voiced desire to get into Parliament so that he could pursue politics in safer and surer conditions.

Disraeli had now established one feature of his life which remained constantly with him until he was nearly sixty – a state of chronic indebtedness, for which his only initial responsibility was unlucky investment. Temperamentally, and on account of his wealthy family background, he was abler than a great many people to cope with such a problem. But his expensive tastes and natural extravagance, necessary in his view to create a stir in the world, caused him continually to enlarge the amount of his owings. He could not avoid some medical effects caused by his debts and other problems which beset him, and his prolonged period of nervous depression in the later 1820s was probably brought on by these set-backs. Especially fearful, to someone with political ambitions, was the thought of being arrested for debt, perhaps at a particularly embarrassing moment such as after an impressive speech he had just delivered at a meeting.[9] A spell in the Marshalsea, the famous debtors' prison, would put paid to any hopes of a political career, while, on the other hand, entry to the Commons would gain him immunity from being 'nabbed' for debt. Not the least ingredient in his desire to be elected to Parliament was the enticement of this immunity.

In time he became convinced that large indebtedness was almost a virtue. He saw the need for continual management of his debts and for the continual adoption of stratagems to avoid or appease his creditors as developing his unusual personal powers, and giving him a decided advantage in understanding the world and realising his ambitions. He gave the following speech to Fakredeen, a character in his novel *Tancred*:

> What should I be without my debts, dear companions of my life that never desert me? All my knowledge of human nature is owing to them; it is in managing my affairs that I have sounded the depths of the human heart, recognised all the combinations of character, developed my own powers, and mastered the resources of others . . . among my creditors I have disciplined that diplomatic ability that shall some day confound and control cabinets. Oh, my debts, I feel your presence like that of guardian angels! If I be lazy you prick me to action; if elate, you subdue me to reflection; and thus it is that you alone can secure that continuous yet controlled energy which conquers mankind.[10]

Along with indebtedness went literary activity. As in the cases of Scott and Balzac, writing and publishing were spurred on by the need to satisfy creditors. Disraeli's first novel, a political satire entitled *Aylmer Papillion*, had been completed in 1824 but had probably been destroyed by Murray on Disraeli's urging after Murray had failed to find any praise for it. In 1826 Disraeli published the first part of his second novel, *Vivian Grey*, now forgotten but then causing a stir on account of its extravagant romanticism and bold lampooning of living persons. Among these was his erstwhile employer, adviser and business associate, John Murray. The latter was justifiably outraged, not least because Disraeli was currently helping to produce a satirical magazine, *The Star Chamber*, which was also offensive to him. The second part of *Vivian Grey* appeared in 1827. The book as a whole went through many editions and brought its author considerable financial solace. But it aroused the enmity of influential persons such as Murray, Lockhart and J.W. Croker. Murray's *Quarterly Review*, of which Lockhart was editor, began a silent vendetta against Disraeli, not mentioning his name at all for over twenty years. This was not the way for a youth with political ambitions to make his name. In the early and mid 1830s, when he was striving to enter Parliament, Disraeli must have greatly regretted the thoughtless liberties with which he had contrived to blacken his own reputation.

In 1828 Disraeli published *The Voyage of Captain Popanilla*, a slight satirical novel ridiculing Utilitarian excesses. In 1831 appeared *The Young Duke*, a romance along the lines of *Vivian Grey* ('what does Ben know of dukes?', asked Isaac); in 1832 *Contarini Fleming, a psychological auto-biography*; in 1833 *The Wondrous Tale of Alroy*, a historical romance celebrating mediaeval Jewish valour; and in 1836 and 1837 respectively, two further romances, *Henrietta Temple* and *Venetia*. In 1833 he and his sister Sarah collaborated in writing *A Year at Hartlebury*, a novel about current politics which was based on Benjamin's own experience as a candidate and published pseudonymously in March 1834. Its real authorship was not revealed until it was rediscovered in an American library in 1979.[11]

By 1837, when he first entered Parliament, Disraeli had written most of his novels. But his two best and weightiest ones, *Coningsby* and *Sybil* – the only two which are at all widely read today – were still to appear (in 1844 and 1845 respectively) and were written when he was deeply absorbed in politics. *Tancred* (1847), an oriental romance, represented a decline to the level of his early novels. His two remaining works of fiction were written and published many years later: *Lothair* appeared in 1870 and *Endymion* in 1880. But these showed little if any advance on his early works. As for *Vivian Grey* and *The Young Duke*, Disraeli had long regretted having written them.[12]

If Disraeli had not risen to the political heights, his fiction would be his major claim to fame. It would have gained him only a brief mention in histories of English literature. He receives little more than this in such works today, in spite of having the *caché* of being the only Prime Minister who has published novels (except Churchill, who published one). The praise which Donald Schwarz has given him as 'a splendid artist' has not counter-balanced the weight of criticism from other quarters, either in Disraeli's own time or later. Disraeli's novels are skilfully written, with some admirable descriptive passages. But the descriptions can be dense and repetitive, sometimes dwelling with excessive detail on the luxury and splendour of palatial courts. His descriptive abilities were his *forte* in both letters and novels. In one of his letters to his father, for example, sent while on a continental tour in September 1826, we have the following superb description of the descent into Italy from the Simplon Pass:

> the purple mountains, the glittering lakes, the cupola'ed convents, the many-windowed villas crowning luxuriant-wooded hills, the undulation of shore, the projecting headland, the receding bay, the roadside uninclosed, yet bounded with walnut and vine and fig and acacia and almond trees bending down under the load of their fruit, the wonderful effect of light and shade, the trunks of every tree looking black as ebony, and their thick foliage, from the excessive light, looking quite thin and transparent in the sunshine, the thousand villages, each with a church with a tall, thin tower, the large melons trailing over walls, and, above all, the extended prospects are so striking after the gloom of the Alpine passes, are so different in their sunny light from the reflected unearthly glitter of eternal snows that we are constrained to feel that, in speaking of Italy, romance has omitted for once to exaggerate.[13]

Alongside his descriptive powers, however, his other writing abilities were weak and unimpressive. He did not have the imaginative power to create memorable situations, authentic dialogue, or convincing, living characters who would find echoes in successive generations. His dialogue is artificial and stilted, nearly all his characters are readily forgettable. *Coningsby* and *Sybil* have made the deepest impression among his novels, not because they are greatly superior to the rest as works of literature but because they deal absorbingly with current social and political conditions. *Sybil* contains Disraeli's famous, genuinely concerned but unbelievably simple conception of the country as being divided into 'two nations', 'the rich and the poor'. A contemporary critic, Richard Grant White, wrote in 1870:

> Mr Disraeli is a brilliant novelist ... but not a great one. With a knowledge of the world unsurpassed among

British statesmen and writers, he seems to lack that knowledge of human nature – he certainly lacks that shaping imagination – without which it is impossible to create character, to make personages that live upon the page. In all his books he has not embodied a type; he has hardly produced an individual. His men and women are things of shreds and patches ... made to utter certain words and go through certain actions with a stiff and awkward imitation of the ways and the speech of flesh and blood. We do not remember his personages; and we forget them because as we read his account of them we do not feel that we know them. ... As a painter of character, Mr Dickens was exactly what Mr Disraeli is not. For Mr Dickens's personages have a vitality and a seeming reality that, when we consider what they are, is amazing. For they are mostly extravagant caricatures. ... The reason of this difference can be told, but cannot be explained. It is simply that Dickens had imagination, genius; and that Disraeli has not imagination, and only has talent.[14]

To compound his deficiencies in fictional imagination, Disraeli had the misfortune to live in an age of literary giants, who exposed his limitations by abundantly displaying the qualities that he lacked. Scott, Jane Austen, Dickens, the Brontës, Thackeray and George Eliot provided humour, vividness of situation, strength of characterisation and naturalness of dialogue which Disraeli's novels could not match. This was the more unfortunate in that his letters, in which he had to deal only with the real and the immediate, are masterpieces of terse, witty and colourful description. He was able to master the letter as a literary form, but not the novel. As Lord Blake has said, he was probably 'the best letter-writer among all English statesmen'.[15]

Disraeli's literary powers could cope admirably with the real, but in producing fiction they were hampered by weakness of creative imagination. It was lucky for his quest for fame and power that he was able to embark on a political career, as the difference between his political and his literary attainments was indeed remarkable.

. . .

MEDITERRANEAN TOUR AND LOVE LIFE

From 1827 to 1830 Disraeli went through a shadowy and frustrated period. He managed to do a fair amount of writing, but his recent sharp vicissitudes and set-backs had left him depressed, listless and in need of medical attention. One physician said that he was suffering from 'chronic inflammation of the membranes of the brain'.[16] But simple nervous exhaustion was probably his trouble, his recent fast and hazardous existence having been too much for his rather frail constitution. In the late 1820s he was considering a parliamentary career, but as yet did not try and launch himself into one. He obtained much-needed rural peace by going to live at Bradenham in Buckinghamshire, where Isaac, on account of his wife's and Benjamin's health problems, rented a country house in 1829. This was Disraeli's introduction to the county where he made his main home for the rest of his life.

Towards the end of 1829 Benjamin was recovering rapidly, partly through the ministrations of Dr George Buckley Bolton, a prosperous society physician. To further his return to full health and spirits he commenced planning a tour which would take him further afield than the two overseas journeys he had already made in western Europe. He aimed to visit the eastern Mediterranean lands, an area which fascinated him as the cradle of his race. No doubt it was the prospect of this expedition which so cheered him that he appeared in London society in March 1830 seemingly restored to the fullest health, glittering in conversation and dazzling in 'green velvet trousers, a canary coloured waistcoat, low shoes, silver buckles, lace at his wrists, and his hair in ringlets'.[17] In such elevated spirits he did not, as has generally been assumed, need the presence as well as the prospect of the East to revive him. But his ensuing 'grand tour' certainly maintained his improvement, and, though his health was often poor for short periods thereafter, he never again experienced prolonged depression.

He sailed from London on 28 May 1830 in the company of William Meredith, his sister Sarah's *fiancé*, and was away for seventeen months. The journey took him to Gibraltar, Spain, Malta, Corfu, Albania, Athens, Constantinople, Cyprus,

18

Jerusalem and Cairo.[18] He obtained especially vivid impressions in Albania and Jerusalem. Some of his best letters were written during the tour to relations and friends, entertaining them with some (though clearly not all) of his experiences. Some passages in his letters about his Albanian sojourn were also used in his next novel, *Contarini Fleming*, with little alteration.[19] In Malta the two travellers were joined by a friend, James Clay. Later an able and worthy Liberal MP for over twenty years, Clay was currently, according to at least one opinion, 'a thoroughly bad unprincipled man' who had a debauching influence on his travelling companions, or at least on Disraeli. The latter's family regarded Clay as having a deleterious effect. But Disraeli would only say, in response to their expressions of alarm, that Clay played some wicked games like billiards and gave him much congenial companionship. Certainly he remained a firm friend of Clay until the latter died in 1873. That Clay was fond of games is borne out by the *Treatise on Whist* which he later published. But it is certain that he went in for more serious debauchery than bouts of whist and billiards. One authority states that Dizzy zestfully shared Clay's dissipations, 'drinking and whoring with the best. From the latter activity he acquired the not uncommon complaint which in those days was treated only with doses of mercury, successfully in his case.'[20] The truth of this is attested by a letter from Clay to Disraeli.[21] Benjamin clearly allowed himself sexual indulgence amid his explorations, and paid a syphilitic penalty.

He soon got rid of this physical impediment when he returned to England. A legacy of more lasting significance from the journey was his strengthened attraction to the Turks and their empire, in spite of his admiration of Byron, who had died while championing the cause of Greek independence. At that time, in marked contrast with twentieth century developments, Jew and Mohammedan co-existed peacefully in the Near and Middle East. Jewish merchants were generously treated under Turkish rule. Disraeli wrote to his novelist friend Edward Lytton Bulwer from Constantinople on 27 December 1830:

I confess to you that my Turkish prejudices are very much confirmed by my residence in Turkey. The life of this people greatly accords with my taste, which is naturally somewhat indolent and melancholy. .... To repose on voluptuous ottomans, and smoke superb pipes, daily to indulge in the luxuries of a bath which requires half a dozen attendants for its perfection, to court the air in a carved caique by shores which are a continual scene and to find no exertion greater than a canter on a barb, is I think a far more sensible life than all the bustle of clubs, all the boring [i.e., boredom] of saloons![22]

His continued personal regard for Turkey, in spite of the strong expressions frequently directed against its regime, helped to support his policy in the Balkan conflict of the 1870s, one of the biggest crises and triumphs of his life.

Sadly, Meredith died at Cairo in July 1831, just before the return voyage began; Sarah D'Israeli had one or two subsequent attachments but remained unmarried until her death in 1859. There was delay in Malta on the way home because of quarantine regulations, and British shores were not reached until the end of October.

Disraeli returned to a country where the main current interest was the Reform Bill. It seemed likely that, if he were to seek a career in politics, he would now throw himself into Whig or radical causes. On hearing in Constantinople that the Reform Bill had been introduced in March 1831, he had written to Sarah that it was 'wonderful news which . . . has quite unsettled my mind'.[23] He had deserted his original Toryism (temporarily, as things turned out), and veered to radicalism for a few years. As a budding reformer he saw the bill as encouraging his own political prospects, and wrote to his father: 'If the Reform Bill pass I intend to offer myself for Wycomb'.[24]

After his return Disraeli made it clear that his sights were set on a parliamentary seat. The example of his friend Edward Lytton Bulwer (afterwards Bulwer Lytton), who was not only a more successful novelist than Disraeli but had just become a radical MP, spurred on this ambition. But it took Disraeli five years of repeated electoral effort to attain his goal, and he did so only after he had returned to Conservatism. Seeing social acclaim as an important route to political success, he became a habitual frequenter of balls and dinner parties during the annual London season from

February to August. As yet, however, the young lion was ignored by the highest lights of society. While he was very handsome, gorgeous in his dandyism, and dazzling in his eloquence when roused from his usual subdued and cryptic conversational style, he was appreciated as a brilliant curiosity rather than as an eligible young bachelor who might be seriously considered for marriage into the aristocracy.

One great aristocratic family, indeed, already regarded him with distaste, and this was ironically the very family on which his political success came, in later years, most closely to depend. On the boat returning to England Disraeli met Henry Stanley, son of the future thirteenth Earl of Derby and younger brother of Edward Stanley, later fourteenth Earl of Derby and Disraeli's party leader and close associate. In London Henry Stanley disappeared for a while in disreputable circumstances. While Benjamin, by his own account, made the most conscientious efforts to find him, his attempts do not seem to have been appreciated by the Stanley family, who rather suspected Disraeli (no doubt unjustifiably) of getting Henry into a scrape.[25] The coolness which marked the relations of Disraeli and Edward (Lord Stanley) during the first years of their political association from 1846 probably owed something to this difficult episode. An incident like this did not impress high society. Disraeli had acquired a reputation as a rather *louche* bohemian adventurer who attacked his friends in his novels, and he found it a slow and arduous process to reach the social heights he aimed at.

Perhaps in compensation for the social disadvantages of his situation, Disraeli embarked on a love affair with an aristocrat, Lady Henrietta Sykes, wife of Sir Francis Sykes, Bart. This came after another affair with a married lady, Clarissa Bolton (known as Clara), wife of the Dr Bolton who had attended Disraeli in his illness. Through Clara, a lady endowed with what were described as 'rather vulgar' attractions, Benjamin became part of a little libertine circle which included the Boltons and their acquaintances the Sykeses. Mrs Bolton became Sir Francis Sykes's mistress after she had been Dizzy's, and Lady Henrietta Sykes became Dizzy's new mistress in the spring of 1833. For the next three years Henrietta was his *grande passion*, the focus of his Byronic romanticism, and he gave her name to his love story *Henrietta Temple*. But she must have added considerably to his debts, which were mounting alarmingly by mid-1836, making him fearful of arrest yet driving him to seek still more loans.[26]

Henrietta was a spirited, passionate beauty, unsatisfied by a conventional role as a wife and the mother of four children. Eventually she began to tire of Disraeli too, and took another lover before her relationship with him came to an end. The new recipient of her ardour was the fashionable Irish portraitist Daniel Maclise, a friend and painter of Disraeli, his sister, and Sir Francis. He also painted Henrietta arrayed in gorgeous robes. Benjamin was extremely pained to discover Henrietta's new affair in December 1836. No less aggrieved was Sir Francis when, in the following summer, he found his wife in bed with Maclise. While he had permitted her affair with Disraeli as a *quid pro quo* for his own with Clara Bolton, he drew the line at the new liaison. Suddenly standing on his matrimonial rights, he publicised his wife's conduct, causing her social ruin, and sued Maclise for 'criminal conversation'.[27]

This unhappy end was far away when Benjamin and Henrietta began their joyful idyll. Disraeli seems to have required maternal solicitude from his lady friends, and Henrietta would sign herself 'your Mother' in letters to him. But she also provided other solicitude. She wrote to him at midnight: 'It is the night Dearest the night that we used to pass so happily together'; and enquired 'The dear head is it better? That it were pillowed on my bosom for ever.'[28] She would not brook any jealous opposition from her husband or Mrs Bolton to her association with Disraeli. At one point, stung by their unco-operative attitude, she descended on the Boltons' house in August 1833. She found her husband there with Clara, and demanded and obtained equal rights in adultery – however anachronistic her claim may have seemed in that era of assured male superiority and privilege. She related the event to Disraeli in triumphant if breathless style:

I ... found his cab at the door, which was open, walked in sans knocking and [went] up to the drawing room sans being announced. Fancy their consternation. I really thought Francis would have fainted ... [I said:] 'Mrs Bolton, I have called upon you ... to have an understanding. ... Sir F[rancis] is aware of [my] intimacy with Disraeli. ... I will give Francis the sanction of my presence on the strict condition of his not again violating by unjust and ungenerous threats ties which he himself has sanctioned, and which both himself and yourself *know* have been necessary to carry on your own game. ... Before I leave this House the solemn promise must be given *never* to mention Disraeli's name as a bugbear ...' Suffice for you and I that we are victorious. Madame cried and wrung her hands. F. cried and begged me to be merciful. I did *not* cry and had apologies from both.[29]

Thenceforth Sir Francis was, as far as Disraeli was concerned, the very model of a *mari complaisant*. He withdrew for a long tour of the continent in April 1834, not returning for two and a half years. During this period Benjamin lived openly with Henrietta from time to time at the Sykes's house in Upper Grosvenor Street, London, and Sir Francis wrote friendly letters to both of them.

Disraeli was also inspired in 1833 to diversify his literary talents, and he chose a compelling radical theme, the French Revolution, for a lengthy attempt at poetry which he called *The Revolutionary Epick*. Arrayed in characteristically flamboyant garb as a neo-Regency aesthete, he gave a grand recitation of part of the poem at the house of his friends and creditors, Sara and Benjamin Austen, on 16 January 1834. Among those present was Benjamin Austen's young nephew, Henry Austen Layard (later the celebrated archaeologist), who recalled the scene fifty-five years later in the *Quarterly Review*:

Standing with his back to the fire, he [Disraeli] proceeded in his usual grandiloquent style and with his usual solemn gesture to ask why, as the heroic age had produced its Homer, the Augustan era its Virgil, the Renaissance its Dante (*sic*), the Reformation its Milton, should not the Revolutionary epoch, in which we live, produce its representative Poet? ... There was something irresistibly comic in the young man dressed in the fantastic, coxcombical costume that he then affected – velvet coat of an original cut thrown wide open, and ruffles to its sleeves, shirt collar turned down in Byronic fashion, an elaborately embroidered waistcoat whence issued voluminous folds of frill, and shoes adorned with red rosettes – his black hair pomatumed and elaborately curled, and his person redolent with perfume – announcing himself as the Homer or Dante of the age! After he had left the room, a gentleman who excelled as a mimic, assuming the attitude and voice of the poet, declaimed an impromptu burlesque of the opening lines, which caused infinite merriment to those present.[30]

Disraeli published three books of his 'masterpiece', and then abandoned the ambitious venture. Although he later wrote a verse drama, *The Tragedy of Count Alarcos*, it was becoming obvious that the poetic muse was finding no very promising outlet in him.

. . .

A CHEQUERED ROAD TO PARLIAMENT

Henrietta Sykes not only gave Disraeli a *succès de scandale* to add to his romantic aura. She was responsible for a crucial turn in his political fortunes, which greatly encouraged his ambitions. During the 1834 season she introduced him to Lord Lyndhurst, a leading Conservative and a past and future Lord Chancellor. The fulfilled politician and the aspirant politician found an immediate mutual *rapport*. No doubt Dizzy appealed to Lyndhurst's well-known raffish side. Any political link between them would not, at first sight, seem to be obvious; but perhaps, as a Conservative in one case and a radical in the other, they found a mutually enjoyable conversational gambit in condemning the Whigs.

For the next two years Disraeli was virtually Lyndhurst's secretary and *aide*. Lyndhurst was also friendly with Henrietta, travelled on the continent with her (though propriety may have been assured by the fact that he was also accompanied by members of his family), and went with her twice to visit the D'Israelis at Bradenham in 1835. There is no evidence to support the rumour which inevitably spread that Disraeli was allowing the current or past Lord Chancellor to share his mistress's sexual favours, with his own political advancement in mind. But, while such extreme cynicism can be discounted, he would of course be grateful for any political advantage which his and Henrietta's friendship with Lyndhurst might bring. His attachment to Lyndhurst did not bring him the gift of a parliamentary seat, as Lyndhurst had none to bestow, but it was instrumental in drawing him into the Conservative party, and led to his being adopted as a Conservative candidate.

Thus Disraeli's affair with Henrietta, purely personal and lacking in political content though it first appeared, was an important step in his political progress and eventual rise to power. She played the vital part of introducing him to Lyndhurst, who in turn was the crucial means of winning him back to the Conservatives and providing him with the influential backing which helped to obtain his selection as an official candidate.

Disraeli was much in need of the boost to ambition and the steadier political direction which Lyndhurst's favour gave him. He had already stood twice unsuccessfully for Parliament, and had not nailed his colours to any party mast. The nature of the times, in which the need for reform was widely acknowledged throughout society, meant that someone with Disraeli's awareness of realities would attach himself to politicians who advocated movement and progress. But progress could be advocated through a Conservative as well as a Liberal channel. Disraeli had expressed his admiration of the Reform Bill, but he said repeatedly that he despised the Whigs who passed it, and he began writing anti-Government pamphlets anonymously in April 1832. He was apparently some kind of a radical, but in the 1830s radicalism came to be expressed by some Conservatives as well as by many Liberals.

The question therefore seemed to be, would he be a radical Liberal or a radical Conservative? Soon after his return from abroad he began to cultivate a political interest in his neighbouring borough in Buckinghamshire, High Wycombe (known locally as Wycombe). He stood there first at a by-election, on the unreformed franchise, in June 1832. He made a memorably eloquent speech but was defeated by a tongue-tied son of the Whig Prime

Minister by twenty votes to twelve. He stood again in the first post-Reform general election in December 1832. Hoping for the support of the newly enfranchised ten pound householders, he expressed support for the introduction of a secret ballot, triennial Parliaments, and repeal of the newspaper duties; and urged 'amelioration of the condition of the lower orders'. There was no Tory candidate, and it seemed that some Tories were willing to support him as a means of defeating the Whigs. He welcomed this, and began to speak of himself as adhering to a 'pure' Toryism advocated by Bolingbroke in the early eighteenth century and suppressed by the Whig oligarchy.[31] But the enlarged electorate defeated him, giving him 119 votes compared with the 179 and 140 obtained by his two Whig opponents. There was time for him to try elsewhere in the same election, and he issued an address to the county voters of Buckinghamshire. The address was fairly conservative in tone, condemning the current 'spirit of rash and experimental legislation'. But he withdrew before the poll as two Tory candidates came forward. Next he thought of standing for Marylebone in an anticipated by-election, and issued another address in April 1833, this time more radical in keeping with an urban constituency. But the expected vacancy in the representation did not occur.

By this time it was, not surprisingly, being asked 'what is he?' by those who were trying to understand Dizzy's mottled political complexion. Disraeli sought to answer them in the pamphlet *What is he?, by the author of 'Vivian Grey'*. Without going so far as to explain what he was, the pamphlet did give another strong indication of his anti-Whiggery by proposing the formation of a 'National Party' of Tories and radicals. But the objects of such a party, in so far as they were stated, seemed to be much the same as those of the Whigs; and the pamphlet has been fairly summarised as 'utter nonsense'.[32]

By late 1834 Disraeli was thinking of another candidacy. William IV had dismissed the quarrelling Whigs and appointed a minority Conservative government, which sought to obtain a majority by holding a general election. Disraeli showed his continuing fluidity. First he approached the radical Earl of Durham for sponsorship. Being unsuccessful in this, he swung to seeking the Conservative aid of Wellington and Lyndhurst.[33] When Lyndhurst's attempts on his behalf failed, Disraeli stood again at Wycombe as an independent radical. But this time he received, through the initiative of Lyndhurst, five hundred pounds from Conservative party funds – an indication not only that it was in Conservative interests to divide the Liberals but that the Conservatives were prepared to woo Disraeli. Irish questions were to the fore. Disraeli advocated the abolition of tithes paid to the Church of Ireland but opposed the current radical demand for parliamentary appropriation of that Church's funds. He also supported, in the interests of English and Welsh Dissenters, reform of the marriage law and abolition of compulsory church rates. He advocated, moreover, reform in the Church of England, reform of municipal corporations, and assistance to agriculture by repealing the malt tax. Altogether, this collection of aims was moderately radical. His Conservative support, however, was seen at work when he said that Peel's ministry was likely to carry some reforms and should be given the chance to succeed. Moreover, in a significant revelation of his attitude to principles and policy, he countered accusations of inconsistency by saying that a politician should advocate policies he thought were needed at a particular juncture rather than concerning himself with longer prospects. This was indeed prophetic of Disraeli's general approach to policy, but he only met defeat again for his pains, taking third place to the same Whig opponents as before.

This election was the last in which Disraeli stood as an independent, 'non-party' candidate, though in view of the Conservative money he had received he had been only partially non-party. After his fresh defeat and the party help he had obtained, he decided to strengthen his prospects by aligning with the Conservatives and getting the backing of their organisation. Thus he reverted to his Conservative allegiance of the 1820s. As soon as he heard the news of his defeat, on 7 January 1835, he wrote to the Duke of Wellington (whom he had met): 'your Grace may count upon me who seeks no greater satisfaction than that of serving a great man'.[34] He applied for membership of the recently established Carlton Club, the central Conservative institution, but was not elected until March 1836.

The Conservatives, who had obtained more seats in the general election but were nonetheless defeated, left office after parliamentary reverses in April 1835, and the Whigs returned to power. Lord Melbourne, the restored Prime Minister, made an unsuccessful attempt, in which Disraeli played a central role, to effect a coalition with some Conservatives.[35] The appointment of Henry Labouchere to a ministerial post in the new Government necessitated, under the rules then in force, a by-election at Taunton. It was decided at the Carlton to put Disraeli forward as a candidate and to give him three hundred pounds as a fighting fund. Again, however, his hope of entering Parliament was deferred: he lost to Labouchere by 452 votes to 282.

After this contest Disraeli was embroiled in a furious and unnecessary clash with Daniel O'Connell, the Irish nationalist leader. O'Connell had given political support to Disraeli when he fought as a radical, but now that he was a Conservative he had no time for him. Disraeli was badly misreported in the press as having described O'Connell as 'an incendiary and a traitor . . . of bloody hand'. An incensed O'Connell, ignorant of the misquotation, condemned Disraeli as 'a vile creature' and 'a reptile', one who was actuated by 'perfidy, selfishness, depravity and want of principle'. Further, he said that among Jews there were 'as in every other people some of the lowest and most disgusting grade of moral turpitude; and of those I look upon Mr Disraeli as the worst. He has just the qualities of the impenitent thief on the Cross.'

Disraeli's blood was up. Unlike O'Connell he knew that this explosion was unjustified, and he prepared to defend his honour in a duel. But O'Connell had already killed a man in a duel and had vowed never to fight another. Disraeli challenged his son Morgan instead, but the latter declined the invitation on the grounds that he was not responsible for his father's outburst. Disraeli therefore wrote an open letter to Daniel and had it widely published in the press. He also told Morgan that he would 'take every opportunity of holding your father's name up to public contempt'. So a duel still seemed on the cards, until it was prevented when Disraeli was bound over to keep the peace. Before he died twelve years later Daniel, who had learned the truth about the matter, sent Disraeli an apology for the misunderstanding that had occurred.[36]

Disraeli, his fame increased by this furore, proceeded to consolidate his attachment to the Conservative party. He strengthened his relations with Lyndhurst and met Frances Anne, Marchioness of Londonderry, a prominent Conservative hostess who became another of his aids to political success. In December 1835 he published a lengthy piece of anti-Whig propaganda, *A Vindication of the English Constitution*, dedicated to Lyndhurst. This was primarily a defence of the House of Lords, which was under attack by Liberals because it had tried to reject the Municipal Corporations Bill. The pamphlet's historical and constitutional arguments are weak and puerile, representing a blatant effort to use (and abuse) history for purposes of party propaganda.[37] But the work appealed to the right people from its author's point of view, namely Lyndhurst and Peel. Disraeli already sensed, in an interesting foreshadowing of their fractious relationship, that he would find it hard to win the favour of Peel. The latter was, he told his sister, 'by reputation the most jealous frigid and haughty of men and as I had reason to believe anything but friendly to me'. But it seemed that he was worrying needlessly. Peel wrote to him in warm and encouraging terms after Disraeli had sent him a copy of his pamphlet, saying that he had already bought the publication and that he was 'gratified and surprised' by its force and freshness.[38] So Disraeli could feel that even the supposedly stiff party leader's favour was shining on him.

His arm thus strengthened, he produced more propaganda early in 1836, a series of open letters to political leaders published in *The Times* from January to May under the pseudonym 'Runnymede'. The fierce anti-Irish bias of the letters suggests that the author was still smarting from his encounter with O'Connell:

> This wild, reckless, indolent, uncertain and superstitious race have no sympathy with the English character. Their fair ideal of human felicity is an alternation of clannish broils and coarse idolatry. Their history describes an unbroken circle of bigotry and blood.[39]

In July he re-published the *Letters of Runnymede* as a book dedicated to Peel, to whom one of the letters had been addressed in these fulsome terms:

> You are summoned now, like the knight of Rhodes, in Schiller's heroic ballad, as the only hope of a suffering island. The mighty dragon is again abroad, depopulating our fields, wasting our pleasant places, poisoning our fountains, menacing our civilization. ... In your chivalry alone is our hope. Clad in the panoply of your splendid talents and your spotless character, we feel assured that you will subdue this unnatural and unnational monster; and that we may yet see sedition, and treason, and rapine, rampant as they may have of late figured, quail before your power and prowess.[40]

Disraeli's determined effort to get into Parliament succeeded at last at the fifth attempt – or seventh, if the two abortive starts are included. His success came in the general election of July 1837 (a contest which for the last time had to follow a change of monarch, in this case the death of William IV and accession of Victoria). Disraeli's success in gaining membership of the Carlton and the favour of some Conservative leaders was now crowned by electoral victory. He was, he stated, asked to stand in several constituencies; and he accepted an invitation by the Carlton Club to stand at Maidstone.[41] He was returned for that notably corrupt borough as the second member, after attacking the New Poor Law in an election speech. The first member, another Conservative, was Wyndham Lewis, a rich Welsh coal-owner and husband of Disraeli's future wife.

A fateful step had been taken. Disraeli was not to be known primarily as a novelist, a poet, a lover, a debtor, or a dandy. He was to be known primarily as a politician. By finally obtaining election he had taken the first essential step which was to lead him to the peak of political power.

. . .

NOTES

1. Sarah Bradford, *Disraeli*, London 1982, p. 4.
2. J. Vincent (ed.), *Disraeli, Derby and the Conservative Party: journals and memoirs of Edward Henry, Lord Stanley, 1849–69*, Hassocks 1978, pp. 179, 31.

3. See, for example, B. Disraeli, *Lord George Bentinck: a political biography*, London 1852, pp. 482–507; Bradford, *Disraeli*, pp. 179–86.

4. Cf. P. Smith, 'Disraeli's Politics', *Transactions of the Royal Historical Society*, fifth series, vol. XXXVII (1987), pp. 69–70, 73–4.

5. See W. F. Monypenny and G. E. Buckle, *The Life of Benjamin Disraeli, Earl of Beaconsfield*, 6 vols, London 1910–20, vol. V, pp. 313–31 (hereafter cited as Monypenny & Buckle).

6. R. Blake, *Disraeli*, London 1966, p. 17.

7. Monypenny & Buckle, vol. I, p. 67.

8. Bradford, *Disraeli*, pp. 15–22.

9. Ibid., pp. 87–8.

10. Quoted in E. T. Raymond, *Disraeli: the alien patriot*, London 1925, p. 75.

11. Bradford, *Disraeli*, p. 68.

12. For appraisals of Disraeli as a novelist see Blake, *Disraeli*, pp. 190–220; J. Vincent, *Disraeli*, Oxford 1990, pp. 57–112. For more detailed critiques see Donald R. Schwarz, *Disraeli's Fiction*, London 1979; Thom Braun, *Disraeli the Novelist*, London 1981.

13. Monypenny & Buckle, vol. I, p. 100.

14. R. W. Stewart (ed.), *Disraeli's Novels Reviewed, 1826–1968*, Metuchen, NJ 1975, pp. 31–3.

15. Blake, *Disraeli*, p. 60.

16. B. R. Jerman, *The Young Disraeli*, Princeton 1960, p. 89.

17. Blake, *Disraeli*, pp. 58–9.

18. D. Sultana, *Benjamin Disraeli in Spain, Malta and Albania, 1830–2*, London 1976; R. Blake, *Disraeli's Grand Tour: Benjamin Disraeli and the Holy Land, 1830–1*, London 1982.

19. See R. Disraeli (ed.), *Lord Beaconsfield's Letters, 1830–52*, London 1887, pp. 43–5; B. Disraeli, *Contarini Fleming* (The Bradenham Edition of the Novels and Tales of Benjamin Disraeli, First Earl of Beaconsfield, 12 vols, vol. IV, London 1927), pp. 306–8.

20. R. W. Davis, *Disraeli*, London 1976, p. 21.

21. Blake, *Disraeli*, p. 62; Blake, *Disraeli's Grand Tour*, p. 20; Bradford, *Disraeli*, p. 43.

22. J. A. W. Gunn, J. Matthews, Donald M. Schurman and M. G. Wiebe (eds), *Benjamin Disraeli: Letters, 1815–37*,

Toronto 1982, vol. II, pp. 179–80 (hereafter cited as *Disraeli Letters*).

23. Ibid., vol. I, p. 189.
24. Bradford, *Disraeli*, p. 44.
25. Ibid., pp. 45–6; *Disraeli Letters 1815–37*, vol. I, pp. 212–15.
26. Jerman, *The Young Disraeli*, pp. 264–86.
27. Ibid., p. 192; Bradford, *Disraeli*, pp. 89–90.
28. Quoted in Davis, *Disraeli*, p. 36.
29. Quoted in Jerman, *The Young Disraeli*, pp. 200–1.
30. Quoted in ibid., p. 220.
31. Davis, *Disraeli*, pp. 32–3.
32. Ibid., pp. 34–5.
33. Blake, *Disraeli*, pp. 120–1.
34. Quoted in ibid., p. 123.
35. Jerman, *The Young Disraeli*, pp. 248–9.
36. Detailed account of the episode in Monypenny & Buckle, vol. I, pp. 286–95.
37. Cf. Vincent, *Disraeli*, pp. 18–26.
38. Quoted in Blake, *Disraeli*, p. 130.
39. Quoted in ibid., p. 131.
40. *Disraeli Letters, 1815–37*, vol. II, p. 358 (*Letters of Runnymede* printed ibid., pp. 341–408).
41. Monypenny & Buckle, vol. I, p. 372.

Chapter 3

STRUGGLE WITH PEEL, 1837–1846

.   .   .

PARLIAMENT AND MARRIAGE

If honourable Gentlemen thought this [the response he was obtaining from the House] fair, he would submit. He would not do so to others, that was all. [Laughter]. Nothing was so easy as to laugh. He wished before he sat down to show the House clearly their position. . . . When they recollected the 'new loves' and the 'old loves' in which so much of passive recrimination was mixed up between the noble Tityrus of the Treasury bench and the learned Daphne of Liskeard – [*loud laughter*], notwithstanding the *amantium ira* had resulted, as he had always expected, in the *amoris integratio* [renewed laughter] – notwithstanding that political duel had been fought, in which more than one shot was interchanged, but in which recourse was had to secure arbitrament of blank cartridges [*laughter*] – notwithstanding emancipated Ireland and enslaved England; the noble lord might wave in one hand the keys of St Peter, and in the other – [*the shouts that followed drowned the conclusion of the sentence*]. 'Let them see the philosophical prejudice of man.' He would certainly gladly hear a cheer even though it came from the lips of a political opponent. He was not at all surprised at the reception which he had experienced. He had begun several times many things, and he had often succeeded at last. He would sit down now, but the time would come when they would hear him. [The impatience of the House would not allow the hon. Member to finish his speech, and during the greater part of the time the hon. Member was on his legs, he was so much

interrupted that it was impossible to hear what the hon.
Member said].[1]

Thus ended the *Hansard* report of the most famous maiden
speech ever delivered, that of Benjamin Disraeli on 7 December
1837. From both its construction and reception it appeared
to be the speech of one who was destined to be a resounding
parliamentary flop, rather than the sparkling parliamentary
success he became in less than a decade. In a debate on
establishing a select committee to enquire into recent Irish
elections, the speech had answered Daniel O'Connell by
denouncing some Irish Catholic electoral methods. Disraeli
aroused vociferous opposition from the Irish Catholic members, expressed in catcalls and guffaws throughout his
speech. Added to the controversial heat of his subject
was the flowery verbiage and overstrained eloquence of
his oratorical style, which caused a more general mirth –
some of it perhaps coming even from his own benches. One
observer, Monckton Milnes, said that Disraeli 'nearly killed
the House', and that 'Peel quite screamed with laughter';
though another version has it that Peel 'cheered him in
the most stentorian tones'.[2] It seems that Disraeli provoked
his normally restrained leader to make loud noises of some
kind, though it is unclear whether these were of derision or
approbation.

The speech was perhaps not the utter disaster it is often
assumed to have been, as many of the interruptions were the
natural reactions of Irish Catholic members to his unfriendly
sallies. Even so the speech was bad enough. It was clearly not
the way to begin, especially for someone who was aiming to
make a real mark in politics. Disraeli was immediately aware
of the need to improve. Ironically it was the benevolent
and disinterested advice of Richard Lalor Sheil, MP for
Tipperary and one of O'Connell's chief lieutenants, that
urged him to be brief and practical in parliamentary speech,
in fact to practise the reverse of his recent high-flown effort:
'get rid of your genius for a session. Speak often, for you
must not show yourself cowed, but speak shortly. Be very
quiet, try to be dull. . . . Astonish them by speaking on
subjects of detail. Quote figures, dates, calculations. And
in a short time the house will sigh for the wit and eloquence
which they all know are in you; they will encourage you to

pour them forth, and then you will have the ear of the House and be a favourite.'[3]

Disraeli immediately acted on this advice. One week after his failure he spoke very succinctly on the prosaic topic of the law of copyright – a subject on which, as an author with legal knowledge, he was an expert. The *Hansard* report shows him speaking in studied contrast from his recent gradiloquence:

> Mr B. D'Israeli would be extremely happy if an expeditious and inexpensive mode of redress could be established against the system of piracy that was carried on. He had been requested to give his support to the Bill by some of the most eminent literary characters. It would give him great pleasure if the subject was taken up by her Majesty's present Government, and he would be glad if the law was perfected even under their auspices.[4]

This brief intervention commenced the correction of his parliamentary performance, and he proceeded to develop a solid reputation as a speaker in the House. But though his performance improved it was neither particularly impressive nor very appealing to his leaders on the Opposition front bench. He did not, therefore, appear a very obvious candidate for office when the time came to form the next Conservative Government. In fact he made little advance in politics until 1844, when he began to receive acclaim for attacking his leader.

In the 1838 session he defended the Corn Laws and opposed a ministerial scheme to reform Irish municipal corporations. In 1839 he made brief contributions on a number of subjects, including national education and the Chartist petition. He expressed sympathy with Chartism, as he did again in 1840. He voted against considering the petition, but protested against the heavy punishments given to some Chartists. He also condemned the New Poor Law and its workhouse system. He thus expressed some radical Tory opinions which had considerable support in his party, but not from Peel and other leading Conservatives.[5] At times he appeared to reflect his leaders' opinions, but at other times he opposed them. Altogether he cannot have made a particularly favourable impression.

While Disraeli progressed little in politics for several years, his personal life obtained a much needed anchor and his chronic indebtedness some greatly needed relief when he married in 1839. His bride was Mary Anne Lewis (*née* Evans), the widow of Wyndham Lewis, his colleague in the representation of Maidstone who died early in 1838. Disraeli had first met her at a dinner party in 1832, and had immediately been impressed. He had then described her to his sister as 'a pretty little woman, a flirt and a rattle [chatterbox]; indeed gifted with a volubility I should think unequalled, and of which I can convey no idea. She told me that she liked silent, melancholy men. I answered that I had no doubt of it.'[6] She obviously liked the silent, melancholy Disraeli, and showed a proprietorial delight when he was returned for Maidstone along with her husband:

> Mark what I say – mark what I prophesy. Mr Disraeli will in a very few years be one of the greatest men of his day. His great talents, backed by his friends Lord Lyndhurst and Lord Chandos, with Wyndham's power to keep him in Parliament, will insure his success. They call him my Parliamentary *protégé*.[7]

Shrewd and practical, impulsive and loquacious, unintellectual and given to making verbal gaffes – 'I can never remember which came first, the Greeks or the Romans' – she seemed a very fitting complement to the impractical, cryptic and sophisticated Dizzy. She was also twelve years his senior, and so fulfilled his need for maternal solicitude. They had a tempestuous courtship, however, and Disraeli had to give her a long epistolary explanation of his thoughts and feelings before her distrust was overcome and the match concluded.[8]

He undoubtedly married Mary Anne more for love than for money. She had only a life interest in her husband's estate. This meant that the estate would not be transferred to Disraeli on their marriage. He was not at first aware of this restriction, but persevered in his marital intentions when he discovered it. When they married at St George's, Hanover Square, on 28 August 1839 he realised that he would not be able to pay off all his debts, now amounting to some £20,000, but would probably be assisted towards doing so from his wife's income of £4,000 a year. She also brought him, though again only during her life, a mansion at

Grosvenor Gate, London (overlooking Hyde Park), and the very comfortable style of living which went with it. Through his marriage Disraeli acquired the benefits of a more secure and settled life and a steadier financial position. These were very important in providing an assured domestic base for the activities of an aspiring politician.

The match was a successful one. But, contrary to the general assumption, the couple did not attain the 'perfect marriage' – as is evident from Sarah Bradford's biography of Disraeli, published in 1982. Disraeli dedicated *Sybil* to his 'perfect wife'; and later, when she gave him a delicious champagne supper after a triumphant late-night sitting in the Commons in 1867, he paid her a warm compliment he well understood of being 'more like a mistress than a wife'. She was quite popular in society, and achieved the distinction of appealing to Gladstone though married to Disraeli. But she was very emotional and possessive, and intensely jealous of Benjamin's closeness to his sister Sarah, with whom he continued to correspond frequently despite Mary Anne's loathing of the practice. As well as quarrels over Sarah, there were later frequent rows over the embarrassing conduct of his brother James. There is even a hint that Dizzy may have had a brief extra-marital affair in 1849 with someone unknown; even a hint indeed – but no evidence – that he fathered an illegitimate child or two.[9]

Nevertheless the alliance between Disraeli and Mary Anne was firmly rooted, and part of her strong attraction to him was undoubtedly the unwavering support she gave to his political ambitions. She had complete faith in his powers and destiny, despite the fact that in the world of politics, and not least among his own party leaders, there was plenty of scepticism about both. After the disaster of his maiden speech he did not scintillate in Parliament but did not suffer a significant set-back until the Liberals went out of office in 1841. Well before the general election of June that year he had broken with his Maidstone constituency, perhaps because of its heavy financial demands on him, and obtained a nomination to the borough of Shrewsbury through the influence of Lord Forester, a Shropshire magnate. He secured 765 votes and was returned as the second Conservative member. The Conservatives won the general election by a majority of seventy-eight, the Liberal Government resigned after a parliamentary defeat, and Peel accepted office on 31 August. Now was the time, Disraeli believed, when his talents and presumed usefulness should receive their well-deserved reward, a ministerial post. He was to be sadly disappointed.

. . .

DISAPPOINTMENT OVER OFFICE, 1841–4

'Literature he has abandoned for politics. Do not destroy all his hopes, and make him feel his life has been a mistake.' Thus wrote Mary Anne Disraeli on her husband's behalf to Peel, with whose sister she was friendly, when it was becoming clear that Disraeli was not going to be offered a place in the new Government. It may have been true at that point to say that he had abandoned literature for politics. It was perhaps his reverse in 1841 that caused him to return to writing, producing three novels in the next six years. Disraeli's own letter to the new premier, written on 5 September, was an equally heartfelt plea:

> I confess to be unrecognised at this moment by you appears to me to be overwhelming, and I appeal to your own heart – to that justice and that magnanimity which I feel are your characteristics – to save me from an intolerable burden.[10]

Disraeli was suffering from a combination of adverse circumstances – his overweening ambition and very high estimation of himself; the suspicions still arising from incidents in his past life; his relatively recent entry to Parliament; and his failure to make a strong or very favourable political impression on his party leaders. The reality of the situation was far different from his expectations. As a relative newcomer to Parliament he was unlikely to be able to compete successfully even for minor office with many Conservatives who had already held ministerial posts. If, as was the case with Gladstone and Sidney Herbert, they were several years younger than Disraeli, this was a price he had to pay for entering the race late. Nor could Disraeli, as a landless commoner, compete strongly with great territorial magnates who virtually had to be given a generous share of offices in that age of aristocratic political domination. Moreover, his

diverse and not particularly striking parliamentary contributions would scarcely have convinced Peel that he was
likely to be a shining adornment or a tower of strength to
his ministry.

In view of the sharp Conservative division of 1846, it can
be said that Peel had mistaken his man in not giving him
office – just as he misguidedly neglected his backbenchers
in general over the matter of deciding on changes in
commercial policy. But Peel cannot reasonably be blamed
for passing over Disraeli in 1841. He probably viewed him
as an able but pretentious and independent-minded junior
member who might, if he gave loyal service, be advanced
to office a few years later. Peel's reply to Disraeli on
7 September 1841 conveyed considerable hope as well as
the inevitable disappointment:

> I should have been happy had it been in my power
> to avail myself of your offer of service. ... I trust
> that, when candidates for Parliamentary office calmly
> reflect on my position, and the appointments I have
> made, when they review the names of those previously
> connected with me in public life whom I have been
> absolutely compelled to exclude ... I trust they will
> then understand how perfectly insufficient are the
> means at my disposal to meet the wishes that are
> conveyed to me by men whose co-operation I should be
> proud to have, and whose qualifications and pretensions
> for office I do not contest.[11]

This could be taken to indicate that Disraeli could still
hope to receive office from Peel if he pleased him politically.
For most of the next two parliamentary sessions he did
usually please Peel politically. In 1842 he supported a
large reduction of Protection in the budget of that year,
and a relaxation of the Corn Law. He felt it necessary
to justify this support to his Shrewsbury constituents in
a speech of May 1843. He had, he told them, supported
these measures of Peel because he believed them to be
for the benefit of the population as a whole. However,
if he believed that such policies would clearly injure the
landed interest (including the population of country towns
and villages and the agricultural finances of the Church) he
would oppose them. Soon after making this speech, indeed,

he and many other Conservatives opposed the Canadian Corn Bill in the Commons on just this ground: it was dangerously undermining the Protection which maintained rural interests. This opposition was not successful, but it was the first public intimation of Disraeli's growing disillusion with the Government.[12]

There had, however, been earlier indications of Disraeli's dissatisfaction with the premier and his lack of official position. In February 1842 he told his wife that he felt 'utterly isolated' in politics. He soon took steps to reduce the isolation. During the summer of that year he established the loose reforming group known as 'Young England', a little congeries of backbench Conservative MPs, partly backward-looking and partly forward-looking and perhaps not really sure in which direction they wanted to go. With valuable support from *The Times*, this group criticised Peel's maintenance of the Poor Law and his alleged exclusive appeal to the interests of commerce and industry. It placed more emphasis than Peel on the workers' need for social reform and on their supposed, but now increasingly outdated, dependence on the aristocracy.

Young England was a confused and heterogeneous mixture which did not produce a political programme and lasted only about three years. Its members' views were ill-assorted. For example, Disraeli probably had no real appreciation of the Tractarian beliefs of Lord John Manners, though he did claim in 1868 that he had had some High Church sympathies when he was younger.[13] The group's main significance for Disraeli was to increase his political confidence by giving him the feeling of leadership; to demonstrate his increasing independence from his leaders; and to give him some kind of theoretical base for his defence of Protection in 1846. Unlike the Protectionist squirearchy he then found himself incongruously heading, he could claim to be something of a political philosopher. Young England helped to consolidate his view of Conservatism at that period. Protectionist and anti-Poor Law, this view was markedly different from Peel's. Otherwise Young England's significance for him was ephemeral. The group was not large or continuous enough to give him a base on which to establish powerful opposition. For this he had to look to the much wider, unreforming and unphilosophical ranks of disgruntled Protectionist squires.

A clear testimony to Disraeli's anti-utilitarian Conservatism and his divergence from Peel was given by his novels *Coningsby* and *Sybil*, published respectively in May 1844 and May 1845. Peel's 'Tamworth Manifesto' of 1835, it was stated in *Coningsby*, was 'an attempt to construct a party without principles: its basis therefore was necessarily latitudinarianism, and its inevitable consequence has been Political Infidelity'.[14] It was the assumed infidelity of Peel, rather than the question of Protection as such, which formed the basis of Disraeli's attack on him. But considered in relation to Disraeli's own long-term development in regard to reform, the attack was spurious. He realised just as well as Peel the need to develop Conservatism in a liberal direction. Like Peel he abandoned the Protection which he had previously defended, and he introduced further liberal elements into Conservative policy which Peel may not have contemplated.

In the latter half of 1843 Disraeli and his Young England colleagues were becoming increasingly rebellious. On 10 August, Disraeli took the opportunity of a debate on the Irish Arms Bill to launch a direct attack on government policy and (by implication) on Peel personally. He called for a more fundamental solution to Irish problems than ministers were offering. Ministers were somewhat disturbed by his manifest restlessness, but not sufficiently to entertain the possibility of quietening him with office. Sir James Graham, the Home Secretary, wrote to Peel at the end of August:

> With respect to Young England, the puppets are moved by Disraeli, who is the ablest man among them; I consider him unprincipled and disappointed, and in despair he has tried the effect of bullying. I think with you that they will return to the crib after prancing, capering, and snorting; but a crack or two of the whip well applied may hasten and insure their return. Disraeli alone is mischievous, and with him I have no desire to keep terms. It would be better for the party if he were driven into the ranks of our open enemies.[15]

This self-satisfied letter gave some recognition to Disraeli's political weight, but not nearly enough, as developments revealed.

Disraeli was hoping that, by his restlessness, he had now made sufficient impression on ministers to get somewhere with them over the question of office. He was prepared to give them another chance, and if they had shown any inclination to comply with his desires he might have resumed the party line. But they showed no appreciation of any need to yield to him. Towards the end of 1843 he twice offered them an olive branch by asking first Lord Stanley and then Sir James Graham to give a government place to his brother James. Both refused. Graham and Peel utterly failed to apprehend the significance of Disraeli's request. Writing to Peel, Graham merely considered the request doubly impudent 'when I remember his conduct and language in the House of Commons towards the end of last session'. Peel replied in similar vein on 22 December:

> I am very glad that Mr Disraeli has asked for an office for his brother. It is a good thing when such a man puts his shabbiness on record. He asked me for office himself and I am not surprised that being refused he became independent and a patriot. But to ask favours after his conduct last session is too bad. However, it is a bridle in his mouth.[16]

Far from being a bridle, however, Disraeli used his unsuccessful request as a launching pad for fiercer and deeper attacks on the ministry. The matter of an office for James was really a matter of whether Disraeli could be induced to become more loyal. In view of what happened in the next two and a half years, it is almost as if Peel had written his own death warrant in this letter.

Before the 1844 session commenced, Peel, taking Graham's advice, cracked the whip. He withheld from Disraeli the circular letter which he usually sent to all his followers in Parliament asking for their attendance during the session. Disraeli protested that his omission was a painful blow 'which the past by no means authorized'. Peel replied that he had honestly doubted (implying that Disraeli's conduct had caused him to doubt) whether he was 'entitled' to send the letter, but was glad now to infer that 'my impressions were mistaken and my scruples unnecessary'.[17] During the next few weeks there was some conciliation between them. Disraeli defended the Government over Irish policy. He gave probably his best parliamentary performance so far, describing the substance of the Irish question as 'a starving population, an absentee aristocracy, and an alien Church, and in addition the weakest executive in the world'.[18] Peel described this cordially as 'a very able speech'.

But friction was soon restored, and became the permanent and worsening condition of the relationship between premier and backbencher. If Peel had conciliated Disraeli by giving him his longed-for office, the future of Peel's Government might have been very different, as Blake has suggested.[19] A subsequent agreement by Disraeli to support repeal of the Corn Laws, perhaps in return for an undertaking by Peel to try to amend the Poor Law, might have caused Disraeli to win backbench opinion to Peel's side rather than directing it against him. By this means the split in the party and the fall of the Government in 1846 might have been avoided. Instead of such a development, however, Disraeli came to believe more and more that his political interests lay in defeating Peel, that Peel was a vital obstruction to his ambition and must be removed. He could not achieve power by serving Peel, but only by replacing Peel's leadership of the Conservative party with his own.

In May 1844 *Coningsby* was published, making aspersions on Peel's brand of Conservatism. On 13 May its author voted in favour of an amendment by Lord Ashley to a government Factory Bill. The amendment was to lower the hours for women and young persons to ten per day. The amendment was carried against the Government. Peel, however, took a firm stand on longer hours, which he held to be necessary for the country's economic health and standard of living. He threatened resignation, but this was avoided by the passage of a new bill and the defeat of the same amendment.[20] Disraeli was realistic enough to tell his Shrewsbury constituents in August that his support for factory reform implied no derogation of the employers: 'I do not join in the absurd cry against the manufacturing interest of the country. I respect the talents, the industry, the indomitable energy, of that powerful class, and I acknowledge them as the primary source of our wealth and greatness.'[21] If he defended the landed interest, he was ready to defend the industrial interest as well. There was a clear invitation to commercially minded ministers to conciliate him on this basis, if only Peel could have seen it and accepted it.

A few weeks later, in June, Disraeli joined a Protectionist revolt against a government bill to reduce the colonial preference in imported sugar. An amendment was carried by twenty votes against the bill. In connection with this new upheaval, Disraeli apparently told a Liberal MP, John Cam Hobhouse, at an informal gathering on 16 June that 'Peel had completely failed to keep together his party and must *go*, if not now at least very speedily'.[22] Peel, attacked by both Protectionists and Free Traders over his sugar policy, was seriously thinking of going himself. But on 17 June, at a meeting of over two hundred Conservative MPs at the Carlton Club, only Disraeli and a few others resisted the adoption of an amendment which made conciliatory moves towards the Government. On the same evening in Parliament Disraeli attacked what he portrayed as Peel's despicable attitude – 'menacing to his friends and cringeing to his opponents'. But the debate ended that night with a majority of twenty-two for the now somewhat mitigated government proposals to alter the sugar duties, despite some resentful remarks by Peel which shifted the accusation of treachery, made against himself, to his own backbenchers.[23]

. . .

THE GATHERING STORM: MAYNOOTH, 1845

The most intense phase in the duel between Disraeli and Peel commenced when Parliament re-opened in February 1845 and did not cease until Peel was driven from office sixteen months later. There was no doubt now that the gloves were off. Superficial courtesies and spells of seeming conciliation no longer interrupted what was becoming open, relentless, and highly personal hostility. Disraeli's consistent theme in his attacks was that Peel was betraying the principles on which he and his party had been elected in 1841. He said in the Commons on 28 February 1845:

I was sent to swell a Tory majority – to support a Tory ministry. Whether a Tory Ministry exists or not I do not intend to decide; but I am bound to believe that the Tory majority still remains, and therefore I do not

think that it is the majority that should cross the House
but only the Ministry.[24]

It was the controversial anti-Protectionist budget of February 1845 which gave Disraeli the opportunity for this
denunciation. In March the fateful Corn Laws were the
subject of the duel. Peel, who might well have been contemp-
lating repeal of the laws ever since he had relaxed the sliding
scale of duties on imported corn in 1842, now practically
signified his conversion to repeal. In response to a powerful
repeal speech by Cobden, he turned to Sidney Herbert, one
of his junior ministers and promising young men (unlike
the rather older and distinctly unpromising Disraeli), and
said: '*you* must answer this, for I cannot'. Herbert made a
speech in which he accused Peel's Conservative opponents
of 'whining' for Protection. Disraeli scented the chance to
ridicule both Peel and Herbert. Speaking a few nights later,
he rose memorably to the opportunity:

> My hon. Friends reproach the hon. Gentleman. The
> right hon. Gentleman does what he can to keep them
> quiet; he sometimes takes refuge in arrogant silence,
> and sometimes he treats them with haughty frigidity;
> and if they knew anything of human nature they
> would take the hint and shut their mouths. But they
> won't. And then what happens? What happens in all
> such circumstances? The right hon. Gentleman, being
> compelled to interfere, sends down his valet who says
> in the genteelest manner 'we can have no whining
> here'.[25]

He then moved from a semi-humorous onslaught to a more
direct one:

> Dissolve if you please the Parliament you have betrayed
> and appeal to the people who, I believe, mistrust you.
> For me there remains this at least – the opportunity of
> expressing thus publicly my belief that a Conservative
> Government is an organized hypocrisy.[26]

The main contribution to the threat of Conservative
disintegration in the 1845 session, however, was over Peel's
Maynooth grant.[27] This was an important part of his policy
of trying to pacify Ireland and defeat O'Connell's movement

to repeal the Union. Under a government bill Maynooth College, the leading Irish seminary for the training of priests, would have its annually renewable grant of £9,000 enhanced to a permanent annual subvention of £26,000, and receive a single additional grant of £30,000 for new buildings. Disraeli – unlike his Young England colleagues Lord John Manners and George Smythe – joined the ultra-Protestants in opposing the grant, though he was happy to continue it later when he was in office. Disraeli's attitude to the question in 1845 represented no consistent opposition to Irish Catholic interests on his part, but was merely the seizure of another chance to attack Peel. An episode which illustrated the dissolution of Young England took the growing bitterness between Peel and Disraeli to a new height. The latter now indicted the premier as 'something ... as fatal in the political world as it has been in the landed world of Ireland – we have a great Parliamentary middleman (immense cheering)':

> It is well known what a middleman is; he is a man who bamboozles one party, and plunders the other (great laughter), till, having obtained a position to which he is not entitled, he cries out, 'Let us have no party questions, but fixity of tenure'. I want to have a commission issued to inquire into the tenure by which Downing Street is held. I want to know whether the conditions of entry have been complied with.

He concluded this barbed and powerful oration as follows:

> ... let us tell persons in high places that cunning is not caution, and that habitual perfidy is not high policy of state. ... Let us bring back to this House that which it has for so long a time past been without – the legitimate influence and salutary check of a constitutional Opposition. ... Let us do it at once in the only way in which it can be done, by dethroning this dynasty of deception, by putting an end to the intolerable yoke of official despotism and Parliamentary imposture. (Loud cheers).[28]

Maynooth demonstrated the gathering Conservative division more clearly than any previous crisis. In the third division on the bill in the Commons, Peel just fell short of having a majority of his own party. But with the aid of Liberal votes (although the Liberals themselves were divided on the issue) he obtained comfortable majorities, and the bill passed. As yet there was no sign of his being toppled. Charles Greville, the diarist, commented after the 1845 session:

> The Session of Parliament has ended, leaving Peel quite as powerful, or more so, than he was at the beginning of it. . . . On the other hand, everything like enthusiasm for Peel is extinguished; the Tories hate, fear, but do not dare oppose him . . . odious as Peel's conduct is to them, and alarming as his principles are, they still think they are better off, and on the whole less in danger with him than with any other Ministry that can be formed. . . . Everybody expects that he means to go on, and in the end knock the Corn Laws on the head, and endow the R.C. Church; but nobody knows how or when he will do these things.[29]

Events soon decided when and how he would attack the Corn Laws, and the next session showed how he would be overturned in the process. The now bitter feud between Disraeli and Peel reached its conclusion amid these developments, and Peel was not the victor.

．　．　．

THE THICK OF THE STORM: CORN LAW REPEAL, 1846

'Rotten potatoes have done it all; they put Peel in his damned fright'. The Duke of Wellington's famous dictum underestimated both the potato, whose demonstrated importance to Ireland in the autumn of 1845 was treated with insufficient gravity in this statement, and Peel, who showed calm determination in seizing the political opportunity provided by 'rotten potatoes'. The severe curtailment of the national diet, lasting for several years from 1845, starved many Irish and drove a great many more to emigrate in a great wave of enforced departure which, sustained by later agricultural crises, reduced the Irish population from eight and a half millions in early 1845 to four and a half by the 1880s. Peel was already well experienced in finding ways to combat anti-Union campaigns in Ireland. He now took an obvious chance to find another, seeing the opportunity to repeal the Corn Laws, a policy he had probably contemplated since 1842; and, at the same time, to try to utilise the Irish crisis in order to overcome divisions in his party and restore the unity of 1841. Repeal of the Corn Laws could do little or nothing for Ireland. It could not replenish food supplies because of the transport difficulties in importing corn from abroad, and the Government did not stop the export of Irish corn to Britain.[30] Irish contentment with the Union and Conservative unity behind Peel's economic policy were to be built on nothing stronger than a symbol. It did not prove enough to sustain these ambitious objects.

Peel's hopes were defeated. Conservative fractiousness filled the period from December 1845 to July 1846. Lord John Russell, the Liberal leader, announced to his Edinburgh constituents in November 1845 that he and his party advocated repeal of the Corn Laws. Peel also decided to adopt repeal by the beginning of December. He hoped that all Conservatives would support him – Protectionists yielding their desires and principles to the emergency conditions in Ireland – and he could count on Liberal assistance. Even if there were a substantial Conservative defection, the combination of Peelites and Liberals would be enough to carry repeal in the Commons. At first it seemed that the defection might not be large. Lord Stanley and the Duke of Buccleuch resigned from the Cabinet. Following this, Peel demitted office himself on 6 December, giving the Liberals a chance to form a ministry. Russell, however, was most reluctant to take the chance. It was not until 18 December that he made a definite attempt, and he abandoned it the following day because of ill-feeling between some of his colleagues. On 20 December Peel returned to office, having declared that he would repeal the Corn Laws in the coming session. Peel, it appeared, had got over yet another obstacle in his attempts to control his difficult party. It seemed that Disraeli was badly mistaken in writing to Lord Palmerston from Paris on 14 December that Peel was finished, and that 'the great object of my political life is now achieved'.[31]

Only six months were to pass, however, before Disraeli could make this statement without any possibility of contradiction. Peel omitted to try to strengthen himself and his

policy by holding a general election. He persisted optimistically with the same, mainly Protectionist, forces that had
been elected in 1841. But he was deluded if he hoped for
majority support from them. Opposition to Peel and repeal
formed strongly on the Conservative backbenches. If some
former opponents such as George Smythe now decided to
support Peel, Disraeli showed no inclination to do likewise
but again took up a prominent position of antagonism
to the premier. He was not at all impressed with Peel's
'heroic', 'non-party' stand. He chose to see this rather as
the vainglorious boasting of a mediocrity. He told Lord
John Manners:

> He is so vain that he wants to figure in history as the
> settler of all the great questions; but a Parliamentary
> constitution is not favourable to such ambitions: things
> must be done by parties, not by persons using parties
> as tools – especially men without imagination or any
> inspiring qualities, or who, rather, offer you duplicity
> instead of inspiration.[32]

There was nothing here about 'the knight of Rhodes', of
'splendid talents and spotless character', who was to be 'the
only hope of a suffering island' against 'the mighty dragon',
as Peel had been in 1836, according to Disraeli at that time.[33]

In the repeal crisis Disraeli was the most ambitious politician who opposed Peel. The difference between him and
other notably aspiring Conservatives was that they sat on the
front bench and supported Peel as ministerial colleagues, a
position which Disraeli had longed for but had been denied.
The presence of his political skill and determination on the
premier's side might have prevented a serious split in the
party. As things were, these valuable qualities were directed
against Peel, and Disraeli's denunciations of his eminent
adversary were vitriolic. He obtained a worthy partner in
vehemence in Lord George Bentinck, who had been a silent
MP for eighteen years and, like Disraeli, had been an admirer
of Canning in the 1820s. Bentinck revealed himself, to
widespread astonishment, as a formidable parliamentarian,
a man with a powerful, if one-track, mind and an excoriating
tongue with which he repeatedly and violently denounced
Peel as a traitor. He could be liberal and tolerant in his
policies, however, as he later showed. As an aristocrat,

his close alliance was invaluable to Disraeli in winning the confidence of the Protectionist squirearchy. He and Disraeli made a most effective, if unlikely, duo.

Bentinck was undoubtedly sincere in his defence of Protection as an economic policy. Disraeli also gave every appearance of being sincere in defending it. But, with his sharp intelligence and sense of realism, he was probably better able than most of his supporters in 1846 to see that, in the prevailing circumstances of world trade, Protection was of symbolic importance rather than providing a strong economic barrier in itself. He wanted the agricultural classes to continue to enjoy the feeling of security they obtained from Protection. At the same time he realised, like Peel, the importance of wooing the great and growing industrial and commercial interest, which he had praised in public speech. They should be made to see that agricultural protection was not much of a barrier to their interests, and should be persuaded to co-exist peacefully with the landed aristocracy rather than trying to subvert it. In this way a lot more manufacturers and merchants might be attracted to the Conservative party. This was of course Peel's object as well. But since Disraeli had committed himself, first and foremost, against Peel, he urged the object along with the maintenance of Protection rather than its large-scale diminution.

Disraeli's stand in 1846 was, nonetheless, essentially political rather than economic. He currently appeared a firm defender of Protection, but this matter was secondary to him whereas the removal of Peel was of primary importance. His later willingness, indeed eagerness, to abandon Protection testified to the absence of any decided and long-term commitment to it on his own part, though in 1852, when Protection was abandoned as the policy of his party, natural geographical protection was still very much present.

His attacks on Peel, rising to a climax in 1846, were the most powerful series of speeches he ever delivered, not excepting the numerous highly skilful verbal defences he made of his Parliamentary Reform tactics in 1867. The presence of a definite antagonist on whom to deliver personal attacks brought out his fullest parliamentary abilities. As Peel's standing was being relentlessly undermined by Disraeli, the latter's was steadily rising. His highly individual manner of speaking, as described in *Fraser's Magazine* in February 1847, became very familiar to the House:

> As an orator Mr Disraeli cannot be pronounced highly eloquent. He never abandons himself to his theme, but always holds it in subjection to his purpose. In both voice and manner there is much monotony. He wants variety in action, gesture, expression, and elocution – always excepting when he breathes his sarcastic vein. . . . His whole manner as an orator is peculiar to himself. It would scarcely be tolerated in another; he seems so careless, supercilious, indifferent to the trouble of pleasing.
>
> So much for his ordinary level speaking. When he makes his points, the case is totally different. . . . He becomes more animated, though still less so than any other speaker of equal power over the House. . . . In conveying an innuendo, an ironical sneer, or a suggestion of contempt, which courtesy forbids him to translate into words – in conveying such masked enmities by means of a glance, a shrug, an altered tone of voice, or a transient expression of face, he is unrivalled. Not only is the shaft envenomed, but it is aimed with deadly precision by a cool hand and a keen eye, with a courage fearless of retaliation. . . . You might suppose him wholly unconscious of the effect he is producing; for he never seems to laugh or to chuckle, however slightly, at his own hits. While all around him are convulsed with merriment or excitement at some of his finely-wrought sarcasms, he holds himself, seemingly, in total suspension, as though he had no existence for the ordinary feelings and passions of humanity; and the moment the shouts and confusion have subsided, the same calm, low, monotonous but yet distinct and searching voice, is heard still pouring forth his ideas, while he is preparing to launch another sarcasm, hissing hot, into the soul of his victim.[34]

Using these tones and methods, Disraeli easily rivalled Gladstone in addressing the comparative intimacy of the House of Commons, and he could address much larger indoor audiences with power and effect. But he rarely addressed outdoor audiences. This was perhaps a veiled admission that he was not so effective in such circumstances. Compared with Gladstone, who eventually became a frequent and enthusiastic outdoor speaker, Disraeli had a more limited vocal thrust of volume and a generally more subdued oratorical style. Gladstone was very much the preacher – loud, powerful, quasi-evangelical and intellectual, if also convoluted. According to Queen Victoria, he spoke as if he were addressing a public meeting even when addressing herself alone. Disraeli was not a preacher in any circumstances. He could perform persuasively and dramatically before an indoor assembly, but his gifts were of the kind to be dissipated and lose effectiveness before huge crowds in the open spaces.

.   .   .

On account of the critical developments in the parliamentary recess (usually lasting six months at that time), the stage was set for resumption of the Peel–Disraeli duel when Parliament re-opened on 22 January 1846. On that day Peel gave a low-key defence of his conversion to repeal until, at the end of his speech, he underlined his increasingly non-party attitude by saying he would only retain his office 'upon the condition of being unshackled by any other obligations than those of consulting the public interests, and of providing for the public safety'.[35] Disraeli promptly raised the temperature by treating the House to another strong personal onslaught, described by Greville (no friend or follower of his) as 'an hour of gibes and bitterness'. The issue, said Disraeli, was not so much over Protection as over the maintenance of integrity and of loyalty to one's party, and in both of these Peel was singularly deficient:

> Let men stand by the principles by which they rise, right or wrong. . . . Do not, then, because you see a great personage giving up his opinions – do not cheer him on, do not give so ready a reward to political tergiversation. Above all, maintain the line of demarcation between parties, for it is only by maintaining the independence of party that you can maintain the integrity of public men, and the power and influence of Parliament itself![36]

Before the end of the debate another forceful denunciation of Peel, by Colonel Sibthorp, a caricature of ultra-Toryism, emphasised the potentially fractious and bitter nature of the session. The House voted to allow Peel to introduce his legislative plan, which he did on 27 January. He then gave the Commons two hours of low-key disquisition on proposed alterations to other duties before finally telling them that the corn tariff would go completely within three years, after being reduced in stages.

Disraeli and Bentinck, with a handful of others, proceeded to organise a backbench revolt. A meeting of the Central Agricultural Protection Society, to which all MPs were invited, established a parliamentary committee to co-ordinate action by all Protectionist MPs, including the few Liberal ones as well as the large number of Conservatives. At this meeting, managers were appointed to obtain the maximum Protectionist attendance at debates and divisions, and to organise support for Protectionist candidates in by-elections. A Protectionist amendment to the government bill was adopted at the meeting. This was moved in the Commons on 9 February, and the vote on it revealed the unexpected strength of opposition which Peel had to face. The amendment was lost by ninety-seven, because nearly all Liberals supported Peel. Conservative members voted against him by 242 to 112, representing an opposition of over two-thirds of his party in the Lower House, and one which consisted almost entirely of backbenchers. On this pattern of Liberal support and majority Conservative opposition, the bill went through its successive stages in the Commons. But the Peelite–Liberal alliance was unlikely to hold together indefinitely, and it seemed that Peel's fall would come about in spite of the anticipated success of his policy. Greville presciently noted: 'Nobody now doubts that the question will be carried, and that Peel will go out soon after'.[37]

Disraeli was now experiencing clear and substantial parliamentary power for the first time. He was a leader of a party which was far larger, far better co-ordinated, and far more effective than Young England. By the end of February its official adherents numbered over a hundred, and soon afterwards it had two Whips. The aristocratic Bentinck – coaxed and encouraged to good effect by Disraeli –

acted as its leader in the Commons, and the much more experienced, aristocratic Lord Stanley filled this role in the Lords. The issue divided Disraeli from his old friend and patron Lord Lyndhurst, who supported Peel.

Protectionists derided and denounced Peel, shouting and hooting like inflamed fox-hunters. 'They hunt him like a fox', wrote Greville, 'and they are eager to run him down and kill him in the open.'[38] Disraeli rarely rode to hounds, but he was at home leading the hunt in this episode. He stumbled more than once, however, most notably when he denied in the Commons that he had asked for office in 1841. On 15 May, during the debate on the bill's third reading, Peel turned on him and asked him why, if he thought so badly of him, he had asked to serve under him when his Government was formed at that time. Disraeli could have admitted that he had applied for office but that Peel was then a firm Protectionist; but this would have laid him open to the accusation of opposing Peel because of disappointed hopes. Dizzy, in fact, was floored. He lost his habitual coolness and rashly stated that 'nothing of the kind ever occurred'. He was lucky, however, in that Peel could not substantiate his allegation until, some time later, he was able to lay his hands on Disraeli's letter of 1841. By then it was too late for the matter to have much effect, and in any case it must have been doubtful whether the revelation of private correspondence and of his own error in 1841 would redound wholly to Peel's advantage.[39]

Following this sharp exchange between the two antagonists, the repeal bill passed the Commons by 327 votes to 229 on 16 May. The bill slipped much more easily through the Lords. Wellington was able to marshal many of the Conservative peers in Peel's favour; the Conservative Protectionists led by Stanley were not numerous enough to sway the balance as the Liberals, though many of them disliked the bill, were persuaded by Russell to support it. On 28 May the measure passed its second reading in the Upper House by 211 to 164.

The last act was still to come. The political factions re-formed in order to drive Peel from office. He had exceeded his usefulness to the Liberals, who now opposed a Protection of Life Bill (or 'coercion' bill as its opponents dubbed it), which aimed to reduce the agrarian outrages occurring in famine-stricken Ireland. This long-delayed measure had originated before the end of 1845. It was introduced in the Lords and passed that House in March. Brought into the Commons on 30 March, it was held up through April by the objections and obstruction of the Irish Liberals.[40] Disraeli saw political value in the bill as a means of overthrowing Peel, but it was some time before many Protectionists agreed with this view. Disraeli abstained from voting on the first reading of the bill in the Commons on 1 May, but Bentinck and most of his followers voted in favour of it. However, some Protectionists, and notably Bentinck, came round to accept Disraeli's policy of opposing the measure. On 5 June Bentinck told Disraeli that they should make this issue one of no confidence in the Government, in order to obtain the maximum Protectionist opposition to the bill. On 6 June a Liberal meeting at Russell's house resolved to oppose the 'coercion' bill as soon as the Corn Law repeal measure had safely passed the Lords.

Against this new conjunction of entrenched Protectionist opponents and erstwhile Liberal allies, Peel could not survive. With supreme irony, his fate was sealed when his repeal bill surmounted its last hurdle in the Lords on 25 June. On the same day the Commons resumed their debate on the Protection of Life Bill. When the House divided, over a hundred Protectionists voted for the bill but sixty-nine voted against it and seventy-four abstained. The Liberals all voted against Peel, even Cobden who had eulogised in the debate 'the unswerving firmness and the great ability with which he has during the last six months conducted one of the most magnificent reforms ever carried, in any country, through the House of Commons'.[41] Such were the political convolutions produced by the Irish crisis. The bill was lost by a majority of seventy-three.

The next day Peel resigned, and Russell undertook the formation of a Liberal ministry. The Conservatives remained divided for years. Though they became mostly re-united by the later 1850s, they did not obtain a majority in the Commons again until 1874. Although Disraeli gained a great deal of political and personal advantage from the split he had helped to cause in his party, he had to pay the penalty of spending 'a longer time in opposition than almost any statesman of comparable stature in our history'.[42]

. . .

AFTER THE STORM: LOOKING TO THE FUTURE

Disraeli had skilfully exploited growing Conservative dissatisfaction with Peel's policies and leadership. He had
triumphantly settled his scores with his former leader and
driven him into the political wilderness. Peel had become a
decided obstacle to the fulfilment of his political aspirations,
and he had removed him. Peel's ministry would find no room
for Disraeli, and he had destroyed it.

It would be a serious exaggeration to say that Disraeli did
all this himself. The number of Conservatives who opposed
Peel was formidable. Bentinck proved an able leader of
this opposition. Stanley, with his great name and lengthy
and fruitful ministerial experience, provided it with more
prestige, if less action. But without the confidence and
morale derived by Peel's opponents from Disraeli's fearless
and continuous attacks on him since 1844, the resistance
in 1846 would have been much weaker. Without Disraeli's
decision that the 'coercion' bill should be opposed, Peel
would probably have stayed in office after triumphantly
carrying repeal. The events of that year would probably have
been far different without Disraeli's crucial contributions.
There is no doubt that Disraeli was the virtual leader of the
opposition in 1846.

Whether he would ever become more than a wanderer in
the political wilderness, however, was still very much open
to question. His demonstration of oratorical and organising
abilities in 1846 seemed bound to give him a leading position
in the Protectionist party. To that extent his own political
power was dramatically enhanced by Peel's defeat. He was
immediately translated from the backbench to the front, and
to a prominent position there. On the other hand, he was
in danger of having destroyed any adequate power base
for the formation of a Government. His Protectionist party
was in a minority in the House of Commons against the
Liberals and Peelites combined, and it was markedly short
of ministerial experience and leadership material. If the
Protectionists were to obtain a majority, they were faced with
the problem of growth, the difficulties of obtaining more
electoral support in a mainly liberal and urban country. The
negative policies adopted by Disraeli and his colleagues in

1845 and 1846 were most unlikely to increase or maintain their support in the political, religious and economic conditions of the mid-nineteenth-century United Kingdom.

Disraeli was far too practical and realistic as a politician to cling to reactionary attitudes when only progressive ones were likely to increase his support and get him a majority. He had been usually progressive before 1845, but had recently abandoned this tendency in order to win a great political triumph. He had risen rapidly in 1845 and 1846 on the basis of policies which he could not realistically maintain. Therefore he had to return to progress. In future years he did not so much oppose the Liberals fundamentally as turn to rival them in pursuing progressive, reforming policies. The Protectionists would find it expedient to abandon Protection (and their own name in the process). By the later 1850s a Conservative ministry would find it expedient to introduce a Parliamentary Reform Bill in order to create more electors who might support them. Disraeli's followers would be persuaded to make some liberal efforts to satisfy Irish Catholics, sustaining Peel's Maynooth grant instead of withdrawing it and adopting other policies of amelioration. They would be encouraged to bear social reform in mind, being ready, when opportunity offered, to build on Peel's example in the early 1840s when coal-mine and factory Acts had been carried, and on the Liberals' example from 1846 when the Ten Hours Act and the first Public Health Act were put through. Conservatives would also find it expedient to be flexible tactically in order to obtain a majority, not disdaining to appeal to radicals in the loose Liberal combination in order to defeat Whigs – such a move was no doubt pleasing to Disraeli in view of his own radical and anti-Whig position of the earlier 1830s. On the other hand, Conservatives might also seek, amidst the quarrels between Palmerston and Russell in the 1850s, to win the adherence of the occasional dissatisfied Whig.

In the course of pursuing some of these objectives, Disraeli and his followers would become a lot more like Peel than they appeared to be in 1845 and 1846. As Norman Gash has written:

Disraeli's subsequent 're-education' of the party in the thirty years which followed the disruption of 1846 was inevitably a return to Peel's principles since only on the basis of those principles could a party of the right in the conditions of Victorian political life obtain and retain power.[43]

The great irony of Disraeli's career is that, in the pursuit and final attainment of supreme political power, he adopted policies not dissimilar from those of the statesman whom he had so vehemently and successfully attacked.

.   .   .

After 1846 Disraeli found himself one of the leaders of a party which, like the Liberals and Peelites, displayed the continuing aristocratic domination of politics. More middle-class MPs had been elected to Parliament after the moderate franchise extension and the more liberal redistribution of seats in the first Reform Act. But this was the extension of a previous trend rather than a new departure. Pre-1832 aristocratic domination was far from being dislodged by the new electoral situation. Upper-class domination was shown by the virtual aristocratic control of most seats, and continued without any strong concerted attack being made on it except that of the Chartists between 1838 and 1848. The Chartist demands were so extreme for the times that they attracted few middle-class supporters and even, at the end of the day, few working-class supporters.

At mid-century the country could not even be described as a semi-democracy. Such a description could only really be applied to it after the third Parliamentary Reform Act and its accompanying redistribution of seats in 1884–5, when most men had obtained the vote. After this, universal male suffrage had to wait for another thirty-three years, until 1918, and no women were enfranchised or allowed to enter Parliament until then. Decidedly, therefore, Britain could not be described as a democracy before 1918. Even after that date, the enfranchisement conditions were unequal between men and women for another ten years, and the special franchise for university graduates and businessmen, giving them a second vote, lasted until 1949. Only by the mid-twentieth century, therefore, did Britain incontrovertibly become a parliamentary democracy. When Disraeli became a party leader a century before this, democracy had not seriously come into view as a system likely to be adopted.

The traditional chains of patronage continued to operate strongly in both parties in the mid-nineteenth century. Obtaining jobs for supporters, helping them financially by paying their rates, and giving them food and drink at elections, were the continuing stock in trade of the political patron. Thus were the primitive and ramshackle party machines of those days kept going by their skilled aristocratic masters. It was a personal, paternal, loose and disorganised system which encouraged little in the way of party co-ordination.

As yet this paternal and personal form of control was supplemented but little by more impersonal and mechanical forms of party organisation. Even the means that had become established – the Liberal Reform Club and the Conservative Carlton Club, formed in the years immediately after the Reform Act of 1832 – were only more centralised and less personal means of continuing the aristocratic control of politics. The two organisations did establish some branches in the country, but this process of more professional control and propaganda was not taken far until after the second Reform Act and its accompanying legislation in 1867–8.

In 1867 the National Union of Conservative Associations was founded as a centralised federal organisation running parallel to the also newly formed Conservative Central Office. But there was only fluctuating determination to make the National Union function effectively. Disraeli might have been expected to give the fullest backing to an organisation which aimed to boost Conservative party prospects by obtaining more supporters in the country, but he was obviously uncertain as to how far he should support it. He was not involved in the National Union's formation. A few years later, however, he did it the sterling service of appointing John Gorst as its chief organiser. Gorst's energy and effectiveness played a substantial part in gaining the Conservative victory of 1874.

A few years after this, however, the Union fell into temporary decay without any preventive action being taken by Disraeli. The National Liberal Federation, founded in 1877 and representing constituency associations of middle-class and skilled working-class radicals, had a comparative flush of youth. Although it had divisive effects on the relations of Whig and radical, and contributed in this way to the Liberal split of 1886, it gave an early demonstration of youthful vigour and effectiveness by assisting the Liberal electoral success of 1880.

Disraeli undoubtedly valued the work of the National Union of Conservative Associations, but probably did not want this body to become too much of a rival to traditional aristocratic paternalism. He had no quarrel with the continuance of the old ways, acting on a personal basis through the contacts of individual patron and client. He did not wish to affront party aristocrats by undermining their traditional modes of behaviour and control through giving too obvious encouragement to a comparatively impersonal machine. He never had the common touch; and it was appropriate in this respect that he should not have paid continuous attention to a popular organisation, even though it was directed to improving the electoral prospects of his own party. It was somewhat ironic that one of the most popular Conservative associations ever formed, the Primrose League, was founded in his memory soon after his death.

Party organisation inside Parliament in the mid-nineteenth century, as outside Parliament, did not bear much resemblance to the much more automatic political behaviour of a century later. There were party Whips who sought to obtain the maximum voting support on important issues, but there was still a great deal of cross-voting – much more, and on a more continuous basis, than became the case later. Compared with politicians of later generations, MPs in that era considered themselves less obliged to follow a loyal party line when they voted in divisions. The Peelites never formed a distinctly separate party in any case, but the voting records of the members of this group were very diverse, and the virtual abandonment of Protection in 1852 by the main Conservative party enabled this body to win much Peelite support. In consequence, Conservatives were well on the way to reunion after the election of 1857. By this time, the two-party system destroyed in 1846 had become substantially restored.

In spite of the eventual strengthening of the post-1846 Conservative party in this way, it was not able to challenge the Liberals successfully in a general election until 1874. Even then the Conservative victory occurred mainly because of Liberal internal divisions. The Conservative split of 1846 let in Liberal government until 1874, broken only by a Coalition of Peelites and Liberals in 1852–5 and by three brief periods of minority Conservative administration. During the whole of this period Disraeli's main hope of weakening the Liberal party lay in exploiting its divisions. In order to build his own strength he sought the alliance of radicals and the occasional dissident Whig – or, if such an alliance was not in prospect, he tried to make the most of comparative Conservative unity and introduce policies which might triumph through Liberal division. He pursued this line in spite of the incomprehension or the outright hostility he encountered over it from some of his own followers. He believed that practically every political method, however apparently dubious, was justified if it served his party ends of gaining place and power.

. . .

NOTES

1. *Hansard's Parliamentary Debates*, third series, vol. XXXIX, cols 806–7.
2. R. Blake, *Disraeli*, London 1966, p. 149.
3. Benjamin to Sarah Disraeli, 11 December 1837; J. A. W. Gunn, J. Matthews, Donald M. Schurman and M. G. Wiebe (eds), *Benjamin Disraeli: Letters, 1815–37*, Toronto 1982, vol. II, pp. 329–30 (hereafter cited as *Disraeli Letters*).
4. *Hansard*, vol. XXXIX, col. 1093.
5. R. W. Davis, *Disraeli*, London 1976, pp. 56–8, 69; W. F. Monypenny and G. E. Buckle, *The Life of Benjamin Disraeli, Earl of Beaconsfield*, 6 vols, London 1910–20, vol. II (1837–46), pp. 75–90 (hereafter cited as Monypenny & Buckle).
6. Benjamin to Sarah Disraeli, 2 April 1832; *Disraeli Letters, 1815–37*, vol. I, p. 257.
7. Mary Anne Lewis to her brother, Major Viney Evans, 29 July 1837; ibid., p. 376.
8. Letter published in Blake, *Disraeli*, pp. 769–71.
9. Sarah Bradford, *Disraeli*, London 1982, pp. 161–74. For the fatherhood rumours see Stanley Weintraub, *Disraeli*, London 1993, pp. 427–36.

10. Blake, *Disraeli*, pp. 164–5.
11. Monypenny & Buckle, vol. II, pp. 119–20.
12. Ibid., pp. 124–5, 139–43.
13. Disraeli to Bishop of Ripon, 15 August 1868; *Short Report of the Protestant Educational Institute for 1887*, London 1888, p. 15.
14. Quoted in Monypenny & Buckle, vol. II, p. 289.
15. Bradford, *Disraeli*, p. 133.
16. Blake, *Disraeli*, p. 171. 'Patriot' in this context is an old-fashioned eighteenth-century term for a radical or protester. Peel was probably using it as a euphemism for 'nuisance'.
17. Monypenny & Buckle, vol. II, pp. 185–8.
18. *Hansard*, vol. LXXII, col. 1016.
19. Blake, *Disraeli*, p. 166.
20. N. Gash, *Sir Robert Peel: the life of Sir Robert Peel after 1830*, London 1972, pp. 438–45.
21. Monypenny & Buckle, vol. II, p. 233.
22. Ibid., p. 240.
23. Gash, *Sir Robert Peel*, pp. 445–53.
24. Bradford, *Disraeli*, p. 143.
25. Blake, *Disraeli*, p. 187.
26. Ibid.; Gash, *Sir Robert Peel*, pp. 470–2.
27. G. I. T. Machin, *Politics and the Churches in Great Britain, 1832 to 1868*, Oxford 1977, pp. 169–77; Gash, *Sir Robert Peel*, pp. 472–9.
28. Quoted in Monypenny & Buckle, vol. II, pp. 327–9.
29. Quoted in Bradford, *Disraeli*, p. 146.
30. Cf. D. Walker-Smith, *The Protectionist Case in the 1840s* (reprint, New York 1970; first published 1933), pp. 56–60; A. Macintyre, 'Lord George Bentinck and the Protectionists: a lost cause?', *Transactions of the Royal Historical Society*, fifth series, vol. XXXIX (1989), pp. 141–65.
31. Bradford, *Disraeli*, p. 147.
32. Blake, *Disraeli*, p. 223.
33. See above, p. 30.
34. Monypenny & Buckle, vol. II, pp. 316–17. For a much more detailed appraisal of Disraeli as a parliamentary speaker, see Monypenny & Buckle, vol. V, pp. 504–17.
35. Bradford, *Disraeli*, p. 150.
36. Ibid., p. 151.
37. Ibid., p. 153.

38. Ibid., p. 155.
39. Gash, *Sir Robert Peel*, pp. 588–91; Bradford, *Disraeli*, pp. 155–6.
40. Gash, *Sir Robert Peel*, pp. 585–7.
41. Bradford, *Disraeli*, pp. 157–8; Gash, *Sir Robert Peel*, pp. 601–2.
42. Blake, *Disraeli*, p. 243.
43. Gash, *Sir Robert Peel*, p. 709. Cf. P. Smith, *Disraelian Conservatism and Social Reform*, London 1967, pp. 22–4; P. R. Ghosh, 'Disraelian Conservatism: a financial approach', *English Historical Review*, vol. XCIX (1984), pp. 268ff., especially pp. 282, 294–5.

Chapter 4

AN UPHILL STRUGGLE, 1846–1865

. . .

PROTECTION AND THE PROTECTIONIST LEADERSHIP, 1846–52

The Conservative division into a majority of Protectionists and a minority of Peelites lasted for some years, but most Peelites rejoined the main body of Conservatives (then ex-Protectionist) in the early and mid-1850s. The split of 1846 made the Liberals the largest party in the House of Commons, a position they retained until 1874, even during periods when they were weak and divided themselves. Nevertheless, Disraeli's political position had been greatly elevated by the events of 1846, for he had become one of the leaders of a large party. He had now to consolidate this new standing and make himself, if opportunity offered, the unquestioned leader of this party in the Commons.

As yet, Disraeli had obtained increased power only in opposition, and it seemed that he might remain indefinitely in this state. While the Conservatives remained divided the Liberals would be able to hold office in spite of their own differences between Whigs and radicals, between one kind of radical and another, and between one kind of Whig (Palmerston) and another (Russell). If Disraeli and his colleagues were ever to defeat the Liberals, they would have to become a lot stronger. After the death of Peel in 1850, when the Protectionist party had become consolidated and the effect of the split of 1846 on party attitudes was beginning to weaken, they would have to try to draw the Peelites back into their own ranks. They would also see the advantage of exploiting Liberal differences, attempting at certain times to gain the alliance of radicals and of Palmerston in order to strengthen themselves against the Liberal majority.

But hopes of strengthening the Conservatives in these ways were largely disappointed. By the mid-1850s, political circumstances arising from the Crimean War produced the rise of Palmerston to the premiership. He led the Liberals for the next ten years (most of the time in Government), and was able to win considerable Conservative backing – successfully playing the same game as the Conservatives in trying to gain support from the other party. By the mid-1860s it was as uncertain as ever whether a Conservative majority would be attained. It was almost another decade after that before the promise created in 1846 finally overcame the weaknesses, and Disraeli gained in 1874 the supreme position of power from which he had dislodged Peel twenty-eight years earlier.

In 1846 the reluctant leader of the new Protectionist party was Lord Stanley, heir to the earldom of Derby but already sitting in the House of Lords by virtue of a peerage conferred on him in 1844. He was one of the very few Protectionists who had held government office. In fact his experience of this went back to 1827, and 'the Rupert of debate' had been responsible for several important reforms before leading an exodus from the Whigs in 1834 and joining the Conservatives in the following year. Stanley had been a cabinet minister in Peel's second ministry and was easily the most eminent defector from him. As a talented and effective ex-minister and a large landed aristocrat he had a unique prestige in the Protectionist party, which he dominated remotely from on high. Despite his periodic lack of enthusiasm for the position, he retained unchallenged leadership of first the Protectionist and then the Conservative party until he resigned through ill-health when Prime Minister in 1868.

When the Protectionist party was formed, Disraeli was probably the only one of his colleagues who could rival Stanley in ability. But as yet he had had hardly any of the same chances as Stanley to prove this ability. Moreover, Lord George Bentinck had also achieved a leading position among Protectionists by his phenomenal exertions against Peel, and he impressively emphasised his new-found dedication to politics by sacrificially selling his stud and giving up his beloved horse-racing. He was the official leader of the party in the Commons until he resigned in disgust, following opposition in the party to his support for Jewish emancipation, in December 1847. In the following September he died, aged only forty-six.

After Bentinck resigned, Disraeli was still in the peculiar position of being a non-aristocrat among the leaders of a very aristocratic party, and there was a marked reluctance to acknowledge him as leader in the Commons. However, he eventually attained this elevated position through his own demonstrated ability, an important change in his personal circumstances, and the absence of competition. By 1849 Disraeli was generally accepted as party leader in the Lower House. He remained subordinate to Stanley (Earl of Derby from 1851), who led the party in and from the Lords, but his persistent activity and sustained talent made him virtually an equal partner. In 1868 he received the reward of long service in this role when he succeeded Derby as premier with little opposition.

As his uncertain position after 1846 showed, Disraeli was by no means a natural person for the Protectionists in the Commons to accept as leader. His Jewishness is sometimes given as a reason for this, but it probably counted for little. Prejudice was far from absent among the Protectionists, but in a liberal age they were unlikely to adopt racial opposition to a Jew who had become a Christian, who had so effectively championed their cause, and who gave repeated testimonies to his desire to uphold the aristocracy. Disraeli was opposed by most Protectionists, though not by Bentinck, when he supported Russell's motion of December 1847 to allow Jews to sit in the Commons, following Baron Lionel de Rothschild's election for the City of London. But Disraeli's stand on this question was only to be expected. It would have been far more embarrassing to him, as a Jew by race, if he had opposed the motion or been absent from the division. Contrary to some accounts, therefore, his position in supporting the motion was entirely natural. He took a distinctive line in the debate, however, differing from the straightforward Liberal argument for civil equality, and this irritated his colleagues for they could not accept the assumption behind it. He argued, as he had already done in *Tancred* and was to do again in his biography of Bentinck, that the Jews should be admitted because their faith was of special significance, being so closely akin to Christianity:

> it is as a Christian that I will not take upon me the awful responsibility of excluding from the legislature those who are of the religion in the bosom of which my Lord and Saviour was born.[1]

Disraeli thus gave vent to the only public matter on which he felt very strong emotion. But he met only blank incomprehension or impatient revulsion from most of his colleagues.

Disraeli's lack of a landowning background was a great deal more important in explaining his difficulty in gaining acknowledged leadership of the Protectionists in the Commons. The Protectionist MPs were mostly of landowning families themselves and naturally preferred to be led by one of the same kind. For all his outstanding service to their cause, Disraeli was still a *parvenu*. The idea of accepting him as leader was hard to swallow. It took him three years from the split of 1846, and the acquisition of a landed estate, to surmount this difficulty with reasonable success. Not only ability but landed gentry status was needed in order to be comfortably accepted as a Protectionist Leader.

The Liberal Government led by Russell increased its seats in the general election of June 1847. It still had a marginally lower total in the Commons than the Conservatives, but the latter were sharply divided between Protectionists with some 230 seats and Peelites with about ninety. As long as this division lasted, the Liberals would be securely in office if their own differences did not seriously fracture them.

In the 1847 election Disraeli enjoyed an uncontested return for his adopted county of Buckinghamshire. The translation from the borough of Shrewsbury would have had little importance if Disraeli had been an aristocrat, but for a non-aristocrat to move from the representation of a borough to that of a county signified a rise in status. A similar and even more important elevation occurred when, largely through the generous financial support of Lord George and other members of the Bentinck family, he was able to buy a landed estate. Hughenden Manor, near High Wycombe, was up for sale. Disraeli, heavily in debt as he was, could not have contemplated buying it from his own resources. But his father died early in 1848. He left Disraeli a third of his substantial fortune but could not leave him Bradenham, which Isaac had only leased and not owned. As well as his paternal inheritance, Disraeli obtained temporary loans from his bank and his lawyers, and a loan of £25,000 from the Bentincks. Lord George arranged this transaction but died before it was fulfilled. His brothers, however, agreed to complete the arrangement, and by late 1848 Disraeli was the owner of a beautiful estate in his county, which he now represented in Parliament. He had greatly increased his own debts in the process, to a total of about £40,000; and in 1857 the Bentinck loan was suddenly called in, having to be replaced by other loans. However, by obtaining the estate he was more appropriately placed to lead the countrified Protectionists, for, as well as becoming a county member, he had become nearly, if not quite, a country gentleman. Like estate-owning industrialists and financiers, he lacked a certain authenticity in his new position. He liked walking and trees, but not horses and dogs; and the popularity which he and Mary Anne attained in county society was limited by their need to restrain their expenditure. To the end Disraeli maintained an ambiguity of social status, neither simply the substantial bourgeois nor quite the aristocrat.

Lord George had somewhat hastily resigned the Protectionist leadership in the Commons in December 1847, after being told that his vote in favour of Jewish relief was disliked by his party. Disraeli's individual way of justifying his own vote in favour was no less disliked, and so it could hardly be expected that Stanley and the party Whips would want to replace Bentinck with Disraeli. Simple strategic considerations explained their choice of a comparative unknown, the Marquess of Granby, elder brother of Lord John Manners. Granby held the post only from 10 February to 4 March 1848; but there is no doubt that Disraeli was unfairly treated, and relations between him and Stanley were chilly for several months.

After Granby had thrown up his post because he felt ill-fitted to meet its demands, the Protectionists had no official leader in the Commons for the rest of the session of 1848. From on high, Stanley tried to guide party behaviour in the Lower House through his two Whips, William Beresford and Charles Newdegate. Bentinck's premature death in September removed one who had outstandingly supported and encouraged Disraeli. Lord George's capacity for sustained, effective leadership may have been doubtful, but Disraeli appreciated his ability and achievement. He began immediately to prepare his *Lord George Bentinck: a political biography*, published in 1851. This work was not exceptionally biased (it contained a balanced assessment of Peel, also recently deceased), but it could scarcely fail to provide a polemical defence of the Protectionist cause at a time which must have been embarrassing to its author who was then advising that the cause should be abandoned. Bentinck's support for Jewish emancipation gave Disraeli the opportunity to air in the book his view about the special relationship of Judaism and Christianity, with which in these years he seems to have been obsessed.

By the end of 1848 Disraeli had still not succeeded in gaining the official Commons leadership of his party. He continued to be distrusted and disparaged among some of his colleagues. The *Quarterly Review* was still pursuing an old feud by refusing to mention his name. But he had displayed debating abilities which were unmatched among Protectionists in the Lower House, and he was doing nothing to give fresh ammunition to his detractors. He had, indeed, a growing body of support for his official recognition as leader.

But Stanley and the party Whips remained unwilling to take the plunge. They resorted instead to the elderly John Charles Herries, who was born in 1778 and obtained his first government employment as a Treasury clerk in 1798. Herries was undeniably quite well experienced, having served for brief periods in the 1820s and 1830s as Chancellor of the Exchequer, President of the Board of Trade, and Secretary at War. Thus, while as a follower of Peel Disraeli's prospects had been blocked by younger colleagues, as a Protectionist they were blocked by older ones.

In a long letter of 21 December 1848, which was a masterly combination of flattery and discouragement, Stanley told Disraeli that 'as a debater there is no one of our party who can compete with you' and that 'the ability ... to make yourself both heard and felt, must at all times give you a commanding position in the House of Commons'. He had, however, to say that 'your formal establishment in the post of Leader would not meet with a general and cheerful approval on the part of those with whom you are acting'. He therefore asked him to sacrifice his just claims so far as 'to give a generous support to a Leader of abilities inferior to your own, who might command a more general feeling in his favour'.[2] But Disraeli would not submit. Being convinced of his own ability and conscious of his growing support, he would not lose the current opportunity by meekly agreeing to serve under a leader who was patently less able than himself. He told Stanley on 26 December that he would not sacrifice 'interesting pursuits, health, and a happy hearth, for a political career which can bring one little fame'. In other words, it was not service alone which motivated him, but only service along with leadership. He made a veiled threat that, if his claim remained unsatisfied, he might prefer to 'uphold the cause . . . by acting alone and unshackled', implying that he might not be averse to causing disturbances among the Protectionists as he had done in Peel's party.[3]

Herries helped to resolve the difficulty by refusing the leadership, but Stanley was still not ready simply to replace him with Dizzy. Acting on Herries' suggestion, he proposed that a committee consisting of Disraeli, Granby and Herries should undertake the job. Disraeli at first refused to accept what he considered another humiliation: 'I am Disraeli the adventurer and I will not acquiesce in a position which will enable the party to make use of me in debate and then throw me aside'. But he soon relented. He decided, as he told his wife, to accept 'this ludicrous arrangement in order to demonstrate its absurdity'.[4]

According to Disraeli's account to his sister, by late February 1849 he had already so demonstrated his superior abilities as to have become 'fairly the leader'.[5] He had indeed become so informally. But the formal accolade continued to elude him. The 'triumvirate' lasted officially until January 1852, when Granby resigned because of his strong attachment to Protection, over which he disagreed with Disraeli. To Stanley (now Earl of Derby) he admitted his own comparative lack of ability, and said that Disraeli's talents had 'become everywhere known and acknowledged'.[6]

By this time Disraeli had been *de facto* leader of his party in the Commons for three years. He had grasped, and received virtual acknowledgement of, his first major political position. In doing so he had overcome disadvantages which were partly of his own making, but which resulted mainly from the traditions and assumptions of aristocratic political rule. Dedicated to upholding the 'aristocratic settlement' as he said he was, Disraeli's rise nevertheless represented a weakening of the aristocratic political tradition. Moreover, during his career he had to do more than simply defend the aristocratic settlement. He had to do this in conjunction with recognising and appealing to the interests of the rising middle and working classes. The long-term result was unavoidable decline in aristocratic power.

Party leader in the Commons he might have become, but Disraeli's position still depended on cultivating and maintaining a satisfactory relationship with his chief in the Lords. In personal relations the two remained somewhat cool and distant into the 1850s. Disraeli was not invited to visit the main Stanley residence, Knowsley Hall near Liverpool, until the end of 1853, and even then the invitation was issued on a political rather than a social basis. Derby was repeatedly invited to Hughenden Manor but never went, though he did send gifts of game from Knowsley there. However, Disraeli had the good fortune to be on terms of close friendship with Derby's youthful heir, the new Lord Stanley from 1851, as he was with several young aristocratic Conservatives. His personality and flair fascinated them, and their aristocratic deference gratified him. Through his intimacy with them it was as if, to strengthen his own position, he was calling in the young to redress the balance of the old.

There was a fair, if diminishing, distance between Disraeli and Derby not only on personal grounds but also over party policy. For several years the two Protectionist leaders differed over the maintenance of Protection. Soon after repeal had been carried, Disraeli had realised that this act would be very difficult to reverse without the motivation provided by a major and lasting deterioration in the country's economic circumstances. Since this did not occur (and did not happen seriously enough to reverse the Free Trade policy until the 1930s), he thought it best to recognise reality and yield up the fierce anti-repeal stand of 1846 to the march of history – softening the blow to rural pride by advocating reduction of the financial charges on agriculture. He no longer mentioned his hopes, expressed in 1846, that Protection would be restored.[7] By mid-1849, in fact, he told

James Clay that Protection was 'not only dead but damned'. Stanley, on the other hand, was becoming more strongly Protectionist from 1848 and declared this attitude in the Lords at the opening of the session of 1849. When, in the autumn of that year, Disraeli advocated the substitute policy of helping the land by decreasing the rates and lowering the interest on mortgages, Stanley expressed doubts whether it would be possible to raise the necessary budget surplus for this policy by the means Disraeli proposed. Indeed, Stanley virtually insisted that his lieutenant should drop his opposition to Protection. Disraeli had to comply. Having already made a speech at Aylesbury in September 1849 proposing his new financial plans, he had now, at the end of October, to make another in the same town defending Protection. He did not relish his awkward situation, and spent 'a most severe and unamiable Christmas', as he told Sarah.[8]

Despite feeling compelled to give lip-service to Protection, he continued to press, during the session of 1850, his own preferred scheme of reducing the charges on land. He won some support from other parties for this, and on one occasion the Government defeated him by only twenty-one votes.[9] He believed that his policy would regain Peelite support for the larger Conservative party. On 3 July Peel died from injuries he had received through falling from his horse. This event helped to prepare the way for Conservative consolidation, but there had to be abandonment of Protection by the erstwhile Protectionist party in 1852 before much in the way of reunion could be anticipated. Disraeli wanted to draw in the Peelites for his party's sake, but not necessarily for his own. He might have to relinquish his hard-earned Commons leadership to a prestigious Peelite such as Gladstone in order to lure him back, and this would be a major reverse in his quest for power. Fortunately for Disraeli's personal prospects, Gladstone was one of the Peelites who did not accept the course of reunion, eventually joining the Liberals instead.

In 1851 Disraeli was embroiled, like all MPs, in the main business of the session – debates on Russell's Ecclesiastical Titles Bill. This measure, an unlikely one for a Liberal Government to adopt, was intended to prevent the assumption of territorial titles given by the Pope to a restored hierarchy of Roman Catholic bishops in England and Wales, and included also a ban on the long-established use of territorial titles by Catholic bishops in Ireland. Disraeli was personally quite unconcerned about the controversial issue, and indeed joked about it in private. But in public he supported the bill, as did nearly all Protectionists and most Peelites and Liberals in Parliament. But, unlike some of his Protectionist colleagues, Disraeli was not content merely to support Russell's bill. He characteristically sought political advantage by trying to undermine the ministry which had introduced the measure, trying to make his own party look more purely anti-popish than Russell. He attempted unsuccessfully in November 1850 to have a county meeting summoned in Buckinghamshire in order to accuse the Government of encouraging the present 'papal aggression' by their previous concessions to Catholics.[10] He helped to devise a motion which declared in the Commons on 9 May 1851 that Russell's ministry was, at bottom, responsible for the restoration of the hierarchy. But some Protectionists thought that this strategy was unnecessarily convoluted and might endanger the bill, and the motion was lost by 280 votes to 201.[11]

In February 1851, in the middle of this turbulence, Russell was defeated on a radical motion to equalise the county and borough franchises. He tried to coalesce with the Peelites in forming a new ministry, but failed because of his differences with leading Peelites over the Ecclesiastical Titles Bill. Stanley then tried to form a Protectionist ministry, and Disraeli was very keen that the effort should succeed. But the attempt failed, partly because the unsettled state of the Protection question reduced the amount of potential support from the Peelites.[12] Russell resumed office, and Disraeli was all the more convinced that Protection should be abandoned for the sake of his party's prosperity. In this aim he had growing support from his colleagues.[13]

Russell's Ecclesiastical Titles Bill, softened when he returned to office, went through Parliament with huge majorities and became law, though it was scarcely ever put into operation. The Government was not strengthened in any lasting respect, and in some ways it was weakened, particularly by the alienation of Irish Catholic support and by the opposition of some radicals. At the end of 1851 Russell and

Palmerston quarrelled over the latter's high-handed unilateral conduct of foreign policy. Palmerston was dismissed, and the feud continued for several years. Amidst these inter-Liberal disputes, the Protectionists took the chance to form a Government in February 1852. This was after Russell had been defeated on an amendment to a Militia Bill. The amendment was introduced by Palmerston and supported by the Protectionists. Russell resigned in a huff, and Derby accepted the Queen's commission to form a ministry on 21 February.

. . .

DERBY–DISRAELI GOVERNMENT, 1852

The first Conservative interlude in a twenty-eight year period of Liberal domination lasted ten months, from 21 February to 20 December 1852. The new Government, led by Derby, came and went as a minority, failing to become strong enough to stay in office. The new ministers hoped that the disaffected Palmerston would join them. Disraeli offered to give him his own anticipated position as Leader of the House of Commons, and Derby accepted this suggestion. But Palmerston declined the offer, and his stubborn presence on the other side frustrated Disraeli's hope of attracting moderate Liberals into his own camp.

The posts which Derby had been prepared to offer Palmerston included the Chancellorship of the Exchequer, and when he declined to serve in the ministry this position was offered to Disraeli. The latter said in a later account that he did not want the post, as he knew nothing of its technical business. This was not strictly true, as he was very familiar with managing his own debts, and he would have to do the same thing on a vaster, national scale as Chancellor. Derby in any case ignored his protests, telling him with lordly disdain that 'they give you the figures'.[14] So Disraeli complied, and his first ministerial post was one of the leading offices of State – another leap forward for him in the absorbing process of gaining and increasing power.

A number of reasons have been suggested for the seemingly incongruous appointment of a notorious debtor as the country's chief financial custodian – who on the very day of taking office had to borrow £1,500 to tide him over a difficult patch.[15] None of these reasons is very convincing, except perhaps that suggested by G.E. Buckle that Queen Victoria currently disliked Disraeli and would not have to see as much of him as Chancellor as she would if he were Home or Foreign Secretary.[16] Stronger possible reasons are that, as finance was the major issue in domestic politics, a figure of proved ability was needed to take charge of it, and Disraeli had decided ideas as to how it should be dealt with. Certainly finance remained a pressing matter during 1852, and Disraeli made determined efforts to treat it satisfactorily and convincingly, though in the end he was defeated.

The new Government's slender prospects were not enhanced when it became known as the 'Who? Who?' ministry, on account of the old, deaf Duke of Wellington's constant repetition of that question when Derby was telling him the unfamiliar names of those who were taking office. Indeed only three – Derby, Herries and Lonsdale – had held office before. However, although it was weak and vulnerable, the Government was safe for a time. Russell wanted to turn it out immediately. But the Peelites, who held the balance in the Commons, were ready to support the ministry provided it was agreed that a general election was held in the summer and that Parliament was convened in November to hear new budget proposals on the tariff question. These proposals were expected to be greatly influenced by the electoral contest. On this understanding, the ministry was able to proceed on account of Peelite acquiescence.

The Peelites, however, wanted to enjoy the revenge for 1846 of getting a Protectionist ministry to drop Protection. Disraeli, as we have seen, had wanted to abandon Protection since early in 1849. He had clashed with Derby then, and ran into conflict with him again on the subject in 1852, when political attitudes to the question, especially those of the crucial Peelite group, were of particular importance to the continuance of the ministry. Derby's opening speech as Prime Minister on 27 February expressed, Disraeli told Sarah, 'Protection in its most odious form'. Derby was no less repelled by Disraeli's speech in the Commons on 30 April, introducing an interim finance bill, which praised the Liberal free trade budget of 1851. Writing in protest to his lieutenant, Derby repeated a remark he had heard that Disraeli's was 'one of the strongest Free Trade speeches I ever heard', and another comment that the speech was 'the eulogy of Peel by Disraeli'. But even Derby was no monolith on the subject, and showed some signs of crumbling. He wanted to introduce a moderate fixed duty on imported corn, but at the end of May he said in the Lords that he was unlikely to obtain an electoral mandate strong enough to do so.

Before Parliament was dissolved the Government was able to put a number of policies into operation, including the enactment of a constitution for New Zealand and (with Palmerston's support) a revised Militia Bill. Measures were also passed to restrict intra-mural burials and improve the water supply of London. The impending election, however, obtained the lion's share of public interest because the fate of both Protection and the ministry was likely to depend on it. Disraeli's address to his Buckinghamshire constituents would be of great importance as an indication of government policy, and he consulted Derby as to what should go into it. Derby had clearly moved much nearer to Disraeli's point of view, for there was little in the address to appeal to the landed interest except a reference to the possibility of substantial reductions in taxation. Apart from this, the address indicated that the colonial empire would be upheld, the exclusive Protestantism of the monarchy would be defended, and the question of further Parliamentary Reform would be examined.

There was much in this to make the Derbyites more popular – whether it was the apparent readiness to abandon Protection, the defence of what was left of the Protestant constitution, or the hint that there might even be a Conservative Reform Bill to rival a recent renewal of interest by Liberals in this subject. To balance any idea that he was ultra-Protestant, however, Disraeli opposed a demand in the Commons by a Protectionist and ultra-Protestant colleague, Richard Spooner, for an enquiry into the continuance of the Maynooth Grant.[17] So on the one hand Disraeli was no longer Protectionist, and on the other he was no longer against the Maynooth Grant. The two lynch-pins of his oratorical onslaughts on Peel and his destruction of Conservative unity had both disappeared. Peel's policies on both questions remained intact, unchallenged by Disraeli. The two issues had provided him with the invaluable means of accusing Peel of treachery and overturning his Government, but it was now inexpedient to maintain them as party policies. They had become political liabilities. Ideas about restoring Protection had become redundant, and a threat to withdraw the Maynooth Grant would destroy the hope (which met with some success) of increasing Conservative support in Ireland on account of reaction there against the Liberals' Ecclesiastical Titles Act.

The result of the general election of July 1852 contained hope for both major parties, mainly because of a pronounced decline in the number of Peelites returned. The absence of any official government statement on Protection had produced a confusing medley of pledges from the Protectionists. Nevertheless the Protectionists gained seats while the Liberals lost some. The Peelites dropped to about forty MPs, resulting in a considerable gain for the main body of Conservatives, and the nationalist 'Irish brigade' returned a number similar to the Peelites. But the Peelites, though much weakened, still held the balance. If the Irish brigade inclined to vote with the Liberals, and the Peelites continued to support the ministry, the Conservative side would be some eight seats ahead of the Liberal and the Government might be able to last for some time. In order to consolidate this advantage, ministers would have to prove reasonably satisfactory to the Peelites over commercial policy. There could be no attempt to restore Protection. After much wrangling, the benefits of the free trade policy were very widely accepted in a Commons motion of Palmerston which was generally supported by the Government, Liberals and Peelites and passed on 26 November by 468 to 53.[18] But Disraeli would have to make his promised winter budget sufficiently appealing to keep the Government afloat, otherwise the Peelites were likely to support the Liberals in overturning it and the ministry would fall. It was a formidable task for a novice Chancellor. Despite this, Disraeli's young friend Lord Stanley noted in his diary that 'his expectations of success are unbounded'.[19]

The planning of the budget was obstructed by Disraeli's lack of experience of the intricacies of national finance, and by the need to make alterations in the original scheme. His basic intention was to compensate the main economic interests which claimed they had been damaged by free trade

– the land, sugar, and shipping – by reducing the taxes they had to pay. In August he was planning to halve the income tax, but reduction of taxation would require a decrease in government spending. This would be difficult to achieve when a rising amount of public money was being spent on social amelioration. Added to this problem was a demand for more spending on the armed services in case of the coming of war with France, which was now led by the increasingly ambitious Louis Napoleon. Derby insisted that this demand for more defence spending should be met.

So in fact there was no prospect of halving the income tax. To halve the malt tax, however, would encourage agricultural production and, especially when accompanied by a reduction of the duty on hops, lower the price of beer. In addition, it was proposed to reduce the tax on the profits of farmers. These had to be the limits of Disraeli's financial aid to the landed interest. A few benefits, not amounting to a great deal, were also offered to the shipping and sugar interests. As well as cheaper beer, the population would receive cheaper tea through a reduction of duty. Some people would also benefit from changes in the income tax rules in order to allow 'precarious' incomes to be taxed at a lower rate than 'realised' ones.

However, in order to compensate for the decreased revenue occurring through these reductions, it was proposed to lower the income tax threshold of £200 so that earned incomes of £100 p.a. and unearned incomes of £50 p.a. would be taxable, and to increase the house tax substantially and lower its threshold. These proposals, however, threatened to remove a great deal of the satisfaction accruing from the reductions; and some of the Irish would not be pleased by a plan to extend income tax (on a selective basis) to their country. The overall scheme seemed to be proposing, as was not uncommon with budgets, to remove with one hand what was given by the other.

Disraeli's budget was supported by Derby and agreed to in Cabinet. But the Chancellor had to make last-minute changes in his plans in order to find ways of increasing a surplus which the need for increased defence spending was threatening to reduce. On 3 December he made his financial statement to a packed Commons, speaking for five hours though he was recovering from a bout of influenza.[20]

By the end of the speech he was thoroughly exhausted. When a four-night debate on the budget commenced on 10 December, nearly all his proposals were attacked. His opponents of course pointed out that benefits gained from reductions were being wiped out by fresh levies – that, for example, the increased house tax and lowered threshold for income tax counterbalanced earned income relief and cheaper tea. In trying to defend his budget he was vulnerable to the opposing expertise of many financial pundits among the Liberals and Peelites, while the financial experts on his own side, Herries and J.W. Henley, would not give much help because they thought little of his scheme.

The main problem was the proposal to raise the house tax. This would antagonise the radicals unless Disraeli modified it. Was there any hope of coming to an agreement with the radicals, so that they would not vote against the budget in the division on 16 December, thereby giving it a chance of getting through? Not only the budget but the ministry's own life seemed to depend on this. In the late evening of 15 December Disraeli attempted a daring political *coup* such as became typical of his style. He had a conversation of one and a half hours at his London home, Grosvenor Gate, with the leading radical politician, John Bright. Disraeli had genuine feelings of affinity and friendship towards this middle-class Quaker who, like himself, was an 'outsider' in politics and, also like himself, had won great acclaim by the power of oratory. It seems that these feelings were reciprocated, until any sympathy between them angrily terminated in the Irish Church debates of 1868. By 1873 Disraeli was calling Bright 'that hysterical old spouter', but in December 1852 Disraeli spoke frankly to Bright of his pressing desire to obtain a majority, even a majority of only one, on the following day. He promised that, if the radicals stayed neutral in the division, he would proceed to modify his tax increases. But Bright, who was understandably rather amused by Disraeli's ploy, refused to entertain such an arrangement.[21] Derby, in any case, was utterly opposed to the idea: 'if we are to be a Government we must be so by our own friends . . . and not by purchasing a short-lived existence upon the forbearance of the Radical party'.[22]

Disraeli had thus been put in his place by Bright and Derby. In the Commons, on the night of 16 December and the early hours of 17 December, he and the Government were put in their place by the majority of members, but not without a fight. Disraeli rose, to the appropriate accompaniment of a thunderstorm, to defend his budget. He spoke for two and a half hours, fiercely and brilliantly, if too personally, denouncing his Peelite and Liberal critics one by one. He ended, defiantly and presciently: 'Yes! I know what I have to face. I have to face a Coalition! . . . But Coalitions, although successful, have always found this, that their triumph has been brief. This too, I know, that England does not love Coalitions.' Even Gladstone was enthralled by the performance: 'His speech as a whole was grand', he told his wife, 'I think the most powerful I ever heard from him'.[23]

But Gladstone unexpectedly rose to answer Disraeli, the champion of Peel opposing Peel's destroyer. He castigated the Chancellor for not having learned 'the limits of discretion, of moderation, and of forbearance, that ought to restrain the conduct and language of every member of this House'; and used his financial expertise to pull the entire budget to pieces. His personal attack showed that the Peel–Disraeli contest was being revived, Gladstone taking on the mantle of Peel. In this new form the duel was to last until Disraeli died twenty-eight years later.

At 4 a.m. on 17 December the division was taken. The Government lost by nineteen votes, 305 to 286, and on 20 December the ministry's resignation was announced. Disraeli's ambitious combination of efforts to offer something to everyone had reacted against him by having its contradictions exposed. The brief Conservative ministry of 1852 was to be followed by two others before Disraeli at length gave Conservative government more stability by obtaining a majority.

· · ·

OPPOSITION, 1852–8

Disraeli had said that he could see a coalition of Liberals and Peelites taking shape before his eyes, and it was indeed such a Coalition which replaced the Derbyites in government in the last days of 1852. The Peelite Earl of Aberdeen was premier, and nearly half of the cabinet offices were filled by Peelites. Disraeli was neatly succeeded by Gladstone as Chancellor of the Exchequer; and, as if to emphasise their recently advertised political enmity, the two of them engaged in an unedifying private squabble over the right to possession of the Chancellor's robe and the furniture in 11, Downing Street.[24]

In opposition again, Disraeli became dedicated to attacking and breaking up the 'unprincipled' Coalition. He took steps to improve his party's organisation and continued his efforts to banish any reactionary image from Conservatism. He was on the look-out for any possibility of allying with the radicals, the 'Irish Brigade', and independent Whigs.[25] His parliamentary oratory in this period was generally not so effective as it had been in the mid-1840s when he had the unique personal motivation of trying to overturn Peel. But there was no doubt of his relentlessly active dedication to the parliamentary struggle and to the advancement of his party by almost any means. His complete absorption in party politics may well explain his remark to Lady Londonderry in the mid-1850s that he felt no inclination to write or read fiction.

In the realm of policy, as well as giving up Protection (at least as long as the economic boom lasted) and maintaining the Maynooth Grant, he gave much consideration to Parliamentary Reform. As early as 1848 he had said in the Commons that Protectionists were as entitled as any other party to 'reconstruct the estate of the Commons' if they so wished.[26] From the early 1850s, when Parliamentary Reform revived as a legislative issue through the introduction of unsuccessful Liberal bills, Disraeli helped to direct his party's attention to the possibility of introducing a rival Conservative Reform Bill. The object would be of course to attract more voting support for his party.[27] Parliamentary Reform was in fact his most continuous domestic concern until he had carried his Reform Bills in 1867–8. He also wanted to increase and ginger up the newspaper support for his party. In this he had the firm support of his friend Lord Stanley, a natural progressive who was eventually, by 1880, to transfer his allegiance to Gladstone (though he left him over Irish Home Rule in 1886). It was decided to launch a new weekly paper, *The Press*. The first issue appeared on 7 May 1853, and its chequered career lasted until 1866.[28] Disraeli thus did better with *The Press* than he had done with *The Representative* twenty-eight years before. He wrote the main leading article anonymously in ten of the first eleven issues, attacking the Coalition leaders. In November 1853 Stanley, who was already known for his desire to relieve Dissenters of having to pay church rates to maintain the parish churches, contributed a rather embarrassingly enthusiastic article in favour of Parliamentary Reform. The Prime Minister, Lord Aberdeen, was sharply attacked by *The Press* as British diplomacy failed and war with Russia came closer in the latter half of 1853:

> His temper, naturally morose, has become licentiously peevish. Crossed in the Cabinet, he insults the House of Lords, and plagues the most eminent of his colleagues with the crabbed malice of a maundering witch.[29]

The Press suggested that Derby, who had served in the Whig Government which had passed the Reform Bill of 1832, was the natural person to lead a Conservative effort at Parliamentary Reform. But Derby was not impressed by the suggestion at this stage. He thought *The Press* too brash, radical and divisive. Disraeli for his part was increasingly impatient with Derby, seeing him as too passive and conciliatory towards the Government, and perhaps also as taking leave too frequently from political chores.[30] At the times when Derby was suffering from gout (and would spend his enforced leisure translating the *Iliad*), this was unavoidable. But sometimes it might have appeared that he was more dedicated to the racing at Newmarket, Doncaster and Goodwood than he was to Parliament. Nevertheless, Derby remained solidly lodged as the chief power in his party. Disraeli sometimes fretted and grumbled about him but could never seriously contemplate circumventing or ousting him. Unquestioned loyalty to Derby was the only way in which Disraeli could hope to succeed him.

Disraeli wanted to galvanise his colleagues into constant activity, making the most of every chance to challenge government policy and building their party into an organisation which would gather more support and obtain a majority. 'He complained loudly of the apathy of the party', noted Stanley:

> they could not be got to attend to business while the hunting season lasted: a sharp frost could make a difference of twenty men. They had good natural

ability, he said, taking them as a body: but wanted
culture: they never read: their leisure was passed in
field sports: the wretched school and university system
was in fault: they learnt nothing useful, and did not
understand the ideas of their own time.[31]

The actual merits of government policies were of minor
importance when compared with the overriding desire to
give perennially active opposition. In Derby's view this
approach was wrong-headed and unduly aggressive. He
believed Disraeli was too ready to court the favour of
radicals, seeking alliances in quarters far removed from
proper Conservative opinions.[32] Derby's own attitude was
to play more of a waiting game, using any differences
which occurred in the Coalition to try to win over some of
its supporters. This approach required patient conciliatory
efforts rather than mechanical hostility, which he saw Disraeli
as too readily adopting towards the Government and which
in his view was counter-productive. He advised his lieutenant
against consolidating 'by an active and bitter opposition . . .
the present combination between those who have no real
bond of union and who must, I think, fall to pieces before
long if left to themselves'.[33]

Thus Disraeli did not have a united party to back up
his approach to the Coalition. The difference in attitude
between Derby and Disraeli weakened the Opposition in
1853 and 1854 and strengthened the Coalition for a time.
The two leaders were seriously divided over government
legislation in 1853 to maintain the powers of the East India
Company, and their division was made more pointed by
the support given by Lord Stanley to Disraeli's unsuccessful
attack on the ministerial bill. During this session, in which
Gladstone's budget won great acclaim not least because
it seemed better planned than Disraeli's of the previous
December, the Opposition could ill afford to pursue divisive
tactics. In the persistently unstable condition of politics,
Conservatives who were unhappy with Disraeli's style and
approach might look to another possible leader, such as
Palmerston, who was unhappy with Aberdeen's and Russell's
policies and with his own membership of the Coalition.

In these unsatisfactory circumstances, Disraeli's innate
sense of political realism recognised a need to seek more

party unity. In the autumn of 1853 he conciliated Derby
– 'come what may', he wrote to him, 'we will stand or
fall together' - and went to visit him at Knowsley for a
few days in December. There he found, he wrote to Mary
Anne, a 'remarkable' place: 'a wretched house, yet very
vast . . . behind the house is a park almost as large as
Windsor, and with great beauty'.[34] It was unlikely to have
been this generally favourable impression of the Knowsley
estate, however; which caused him to write in 1862, when
there was an intention to offer Stanley the throne of Greece:

> It is a dazzling adventure for the House of Stanley, but
> they are not an imaginative race, and, I fancy, they will
> prefer Knowsley to the Parthenon and Lancashire to
> the Attic plain.[35]

Despite his satisfactory visit, the better party co-ordination
which Disraeli was hoping for did not materialise. Britain and
France declared war on Russia on 28 March 1854, and had
little success for many months. But the Opposition continued
to drift without much aim or cohesion. There was success
in resisting ministerial domestic legislation, but the Coalition
continued in office when a more co-ordinated effort might
have overturned it. In August Disraeli complained vehemently to his friend the Marchioness of Londonderry that
he was left isolated, especially by his leader, to press on with
party business in discouraging circumstances:

> Tho' so many notables and magnificoes belong to
> the party there was never an aggregation of human
> beings who exercised less social influence. They seem to
> despise all the modes and means of managing mankind.
>
>   As for our Chief we never see him. His house is always
> closed, he subscribes to nothing tho' his fortune is very
> large; and expects nevertheless everything to be done.
> I have never yet been fairly backed in life. . . . This has
> been my fate and I never felt it more keenly than at
> the present moment, with a confederate [Derby] always
> at Newmarket and Doncaster, when Europe, nay the
> world is in the throes of immense changes and all the
> elements of power at home in a state of dissolution. If
> ever there were a time when a political chief should
> concentrate his mind and resources on the situation 'tis
> the present.[36]

The Crimean War eventually brought an end to the Coalition, but the Derbyite Conservatives did not take the chance to form another minority Government. The Coalition was increasingly criticised for mismanagement of the war effort, especially the gross inefficiencies of the supply system. In January 1855 the radical MP John Arthur Roebuck gave notice of a motion for a select committee of enquiry into the conduct of the war. Disraeli was keen to join the attack on the ministry. Derby was less enthusiastic but eventually acquiesced, and on 29 January Roebuck's motion was carried by the large majority of 305 votes to 148. Aberdeen resigned, and the Queen invited Derby to form an administration. In a clear indication of the pivotal position which Palmerston had acquired in politics and public support, Derby said that he must obtain him as one of his ministers as he would supply particular strength and expertise in conducting the war. But, after being initially favourable, Palmerston declined Derby's offer, and Derby abandoned the idea of forming a Government.[37] Russell then refused a similar invitation; but Palmerston accepted one, and the task of leading a new ministry fell to him.

Thus commenced the decade of Palmerston, an independent and conservative Liberal who managed, mainly on account of his firm defence of Britain's overseas interests, to unite behind him the support not only of most Liberals but of many Conservatives as well. On the Coalition's fall, Palmerston stepped into the position Disraeli had been hoping to win for the Conservatives. Even though the Peelites who joined Palmerston's ministry soon left it, on 22 February 1855, because he insisted on proceeding with the enquiry into the war effort, they rejoined Palmerston a few years later. The Conservatives remained in opposition for most of the next decade, while the Liberals, after a few precarious years, strengthened themselves in 1859 when Palmerston's second ministry was formed.

It seems probable that if Derby had formed a ministry without Palmerston it would have been only a brief one. But the disappointed Disraeli complained to Lady Londonderry that 'our chief has bolted again'. While he had no doubt that Derby's leadership remained a necessity, he feared that Derby's caution might lose chances of making progress. Disraeli's attitude towards Palmerston was probably one of private envy despite the public opposition he felt compelled to show. Palmerston's *coups* in overseas policy were the sort of dazzling affairs which, it may be gathered from his own later actions, Disraeli would have liked to carry out himself. However, in order to assuage his sore feelings over the lost chance of forming a Conservative Government, he tried to negate the new premier's septuagenarian jauntiness by claiming that he was decidedly senile:

> tho' he is really an imposter (*sic*), utterly exhausted, and at the best only ginger beer and not champaign, and now an old painted Pantaloon, very deaf, very blind, and with false teeth, which would fall out of his mouth when speaking, if he did not hesitate and halt so in his talk – he (*sic*) is a name which the country resolves to associate with energy, wisdom, and eloquence, and will until he has tried and failed.[38]

The new Government soon lost its Peelite members, but the war began to go better for Britain and her French ally. Disraeli wanted, as before, to embarrass the ministry whenever possible. He wished to urge, especially in *The Press*, a definite peace policy. But this desire caused a further collision with Derby, who refused to weaken the Government when it was conducting 'an inevitable war'.[39] When the Treaty of Paris was signed with Russia on 30 March 1856, Disraeli was fairly content with its terms but most of his colleagues were dissatisfied with them. When conflict with Russia again developed strongly twenty years later, Disraeli was ironically in the same position as Palmerston had been, championing the combined interests of Britain and Turkey against Russian advance.

The strained relations between Disraeli and most of his party did not improve over the next two years. He apparently communicated little with Derby, and, according to a letter from Derby to Lord Malmesbury at the end of 1856, Disraeli did not see much of the party members in general. But, added Derby, he remained indispensable to the party because of his outstanding abilities. So the situation was much as it had been in the later 1840s: Disraeli was disliked, distrusted, and misunderstood by many in his party, but they could not do without his talent, initiative, and vigour. Disraeli for his part was convinced, with good reason, that he was not being appreciated politically. When he visited Paris in the autumn of 1856 he was disappointed to find that this lack of appreciation was also registered by Napoleon III. The emperor was reluctant to see Disraeli at all, refused to be persuaded by him to cease supporting Palmerston, and made the singularly ill-judged comment to Malmesbury that Dizzy 'like all literary men ... [was] ignorant of the world, talking well, but nervous when the moment of action arises'.[40]

By the end of 1856 the cause of Disraeli and of the Conservative party seemed in the doldrums indeed. Things did not improve in 1857, though there was more political excitement. Palmerston seemed to be carrying all before him. In February 1857 he managed to get over an embarrassing attack on his foreign policy by Disraeli, who had been armed with information about secret negotiations in Paris by Ralph Earle, the latest of his young *protégés*.[41] In March the budget was carried by eighty votes against opposition from both Disraeli and Gladstone. But a few days later a combination of radicals, Conservatives and Peelites defeated Palmerston by sixteen votes over his aggressive policy towards China, which had issued in the bombardment of Canton. This time it was Derby who was more eager than Disraeli in wanting to challenge the Government, and Derby made one of his best speeches against the aggression. Palmerston accepted a challenge from Disraeli to appeal to the country, and succeeded triumphantly in the general election of late March and early April 1857.

It is too simple to regard this election purely as a vote for or against Palmerston as premier. Other issues, especially an upsurge of Nonconformist demand for relief from civil grievances, complicated the contest and the results. But Palmerston and his China policy did dominate the election, which gave him a substantial overall majority of about a hundred. The radicals lost heavily, and the Derbyites lost about thirty seats, but Disraeli claimed that the 280 MPs of his party who were returned would prove to be a much more united body than before. Certainly the sharp Peelite losses, reducing them to only some half-dozen MPs, strengthened the feeling of Conservative unity; and the Derbyites as well as the Liberals hoped to win the Peelites over. Disraeli wrote optimistically:

We shall now have a House of Commons with two parties and with definite opinions. All the sections, all the conceited individuals who were what they styled themselves 'independent', have been swept away, erased, obliterated, expunged. The state of affairs will be much more wholesome and more agreeable.[42]

The Conservative majority appeared more united than the Liberals, who were still divided into Palmerstonian and Russellite Whigs and into different kinds of radical. But some of the subsequent policies of Palmerston revealed the Conservatives as being far from united. Many Conservative MPs were more inclined to sympathise with Palmerstonian policies than Disraeli wanted.

The severe and protracted Indian Mutiny, commencing in May, provided a strong reason for Conservatives to support the Government during the rest of the year and into 1858. Disraeli, as was natural for an amateur orientalist, was keenly interested in Indian questions, and he deprecated the Whig commitment to westernisation. While he agreed that the Mutiny had to be suppressed, he showed sympathy with the desire to maintain Indian customs and with Indian aspirations for greater political freedom. In a speech in the Commons on 27 July 1857 he took issue with some trivial views of the causes of the uprising – 'the rise and fall of empires are not affairs of greased cartridges' – and denounced the recent aggressive annexationist aspects of British policy in India. In a foreshadowing of his own Indian policy in the 1870s, Disraeli urged the Government to make the Indian people more conscious of 'their real Ruler and Sovereign, Queen Victoria'.[43] This suggestion undoubtedly represented imperialism, but it was an imperialism which attempted, more than some other approaches, to sympathise with indigenous customs and aspirations. In February 1858 he opposed the government bill to abolish the East India Company, but at least eighty Conservative MPs refused to follow his lead and vote for an amendment. His hopes of greater Conservative unity were being challenged.

Early in 1858 the confidence bestowed on Palmerston by his electoral victory was shaken. Among other embarrassments, he had to face a further crisis in overseas policy. This came out of the Orsini bomb-throwing incident in Paris on 14 January. An Italian nationalist conspiracy, apparently founded on frustration with Napoleon III, was fomented in London and resulted in a bomb, made in Birmingham, being thrown at the French emperor. It missed its object but killed many others. Amidst ensuing uproar the French Government put pressure on Palmerston to tighten the English law against conspiracy to murder, so that those in England who were suspected of plotting similar actions to take place abroad could be arrested and tried.

Palmerston accordingly introduced a Conspiracy to Murder Bill. Many of his diverse opponents – Russell, the radicals, Derbyites and Peelites – combined against his policy on the grounds that he was willing to give way too readily to the demands of a foreign ruler. Disraeli scented a possible government defeat. After voting for the first reading of the bill he voted against the second, though on a different point from the radicals. Conservatives were again divided, and the second reading was opposed by only 146 of the Conservative MPs. Nevertheless the bill was defeated on this reading by 234 votes to 215 on 19 February. Eighty-four Liberals voted against Palmerston.

The premier resigned. Derby, after unsuccessfully asking the independent Liberal Earl Grey and the anti-Palmerstonian Peelite Gladstone to join him, formed a purely Conservative ministry. A chance for the Conservatives to form a Government had appeared for the fourth time out of the political confusion of the 1850s. Once again, having only a minority in the Commons, they were in a weak position to meet it. But for the second time in the decade they took the opportunity.

. . .

DERBY–DISRAELI GOVERNMENT, 1858–9

The Conservatives were in office this time for sixteen months, from February 1858 to June 1859. This exceeded by six months their previous period as a Government in 1852; but they did not become politically stronger than before, and when they left office they seemed no nearer to obtaining a majority. As in their previous period some constructive measures were passed. Palmerston's Conspiracy Bill was dropped, France being nonetheless mollified, but his

India Bill, proposing to wind up the East India Company, was adopted by the new Government and passed. In the aftermath of the Mutiny it established a new form of government, providing for a Secretary of State and a council of eighteen. The basic form of the new system lasted until the Government of India Act of 1935. A resolution of 1858 admitted a non-Christian Jewish MP to the Commons for the first time, and this led to a permanent arrangement which permitted elected Jews to take their seats. The passage of a bill to clean up the Thames by installing main drainage would have appealed to Disraeli's interest in social improvement. Back in his former office of Chancellor of the Exchequer, he was responsible for two tight-pursed budgets which made no concessions to a current demand for more spending on armaments.

Disraeli was still much concerned with trying to strengthen his party by winning over politicians who were currently footloose and might be attracted by a definite party connection. Gladstone was one of these. He had been out of office since leaving Palmerston in February 1855 and was reluctant to re-join him as he detested most of his policies. Gladstone was offered a post in Derby's Cabinet in May 1858. In connection with this offer, Disraeli demonstrated that party interest could surmount his personal antipathies and fears of internal rivalry. He wrote to Gladstone on 25 May in generous terms:

> I think it of such permanent importance to the public interests that you should assume at this time a commanding position in the administration of affairs that I feel it a solemn duty to lay before you some facts. . . . Our mutual relations have caused the great difficulty in accomplishing a result which I have always anxiously desired. . . . Don't you think the time has come when you might deign to be magnanimous?[44]

Gladstone replied in a similarly fairly friendly fashion, denying that he had ever felt any enmity towards Disraeli. But he refused the offer. He disliked Palmerston; he also disliked Disraeli. His decision to re-join Palmerston the following year occurred supposedly because of their shared support for Italian independence, but there were, no doubt, additional reasons. As a career politician, Gladstone was well aware that the Liberal leaders (Palmerston and Russell) were older than the Conservative ones (Derby and Disraeli), and that his chances of becoming leader of a party would be more promising in this respect if he joined the Liberals. He would also avoid the frustration which was likely to arise from the internal rivalry of Disraeli. In May 1859, before the Conservative Government ended, Gladstone was again offered a cabinet post, and again he refused.

The issue of Parliamentary Reform was significant in this ministry, as a Conservative Reform Bill was introduced for the first time. The introduction of reforming policies such as extension and redistribution of the franchise was characteristic of the prevailing liberal approach to politics, adopted by many Conservatives as well as by Liberals. The Liberal party claimed to be acting on principle when introducing Parliamentary Reform, but party expediency was a large, if unexpressed, ingredient in the process. Among Conservatives the motivation was, very largely, one of party expediency and advancement. The differing natures of Liberal and Conservative Reform Bills reflected the different hopes each party had of gaining support through electoral extension.

The Reform Bill of 1859 was the result of a great deal of work and argument among the cabinet ministers. A cabinet committee held meetings throughout November 1858 to draft a bill. Stanley, who had become the first Secretary for India under the provisions of the 1858 Act, was true to his previously expressed enthusiasm on the subject by favouring a wide liberal measure. His father, the Prime Minister, favoured a measure more narrowly tailored to Conservative party interest. Disraeli showed sympathy with both father and son, working out plans with them and at some points combining their suggestions in the service of party benefit.[45]

The Conservative party looked to the county seats as its main source of strength in the House of Commons. Under the original proposals these seats would be increased by fifty-two, through a redistribution of seats away from the smaller boroughs. The £10 household franchise operating in the borough seats since 1832 would be extended to the counties. By these means it was hoped to establish an electorate which would be more likely than the existing one to return a Conservative majority. But the provisions were strongly contested by some cabinet ministers who feared the encouragement they might give to democracy. The Home Secretary, Spencer Walpole, and the President of the Board of Trade, J.W. Henley, were especially opposed to them. The bill underwent much alteration in a fruitless effort to reach agreement. The redistribution of seats was greatly reduced, and some 'fancy franchises' (as Bright described them) were added, apparently at Disraeli's suggestion. These minor indicators of the importance of property in qualifying for the vote proposed to enfranchise, among other categories, possessors of £60 in a savings bank and government pensioners receiving £20 a year or more.

The strenuous effort to preserve government unity was to no avail. Disraeli did his best for the measure, introducing it with an impressive speech in the Commons on 28 February 1859. But Walpole and Henley spoke against it, and both resigned from the ministry in protest. The visible Conservative disunity encouraged opposition from other quarters. Disraeli had doubtless hoped to pick up enough Liberal support to get the bill through, but he was disappointed. The radicals found both the enfranchisement and redistribution sections too narrow and one-sided. They wanted to extend the vote on a substantial scale to the urban working class. The Liberal party as a whole looked askance at a bill which was shaped with the intention of increasing the Conservative vote. Whereas the Conservatives had split over the measure, the Liberals came together to oppose it. Palmerston and Russell began to terminate their lengthy period of fractious dispute and to contemplate forming a ministry together. Russell drafted a resolution against aspects of the bill which, although Gladstone supported the Government against it, was carried by 330 votes to 291 on 31 March. The bill was dead.

The Cabinet decided on a dissolution of Parliament, which was announced on 4 April. A general election would commence on the twenty-ninth. Disraeli, sanguine as usual about his party's prospects, thought the Conservatives might gain as many as sixty seats. They gained only about half that number, and had a new total of 307.[46] They were still considerably short of the much-desired majority. Indeed, they could be regarded as being stuck in a minority rut, as they had oscillated within totals only fifty seats apart over four general elections since 1846. The Liberals, for their part, held on to a reduced but useful majority of forty. This proved enough to keep them in office for six years, after which they obtained yet another majority.

As the elections were turning out not very satisfactorily for the Conservative Government, Disraeli looked again for help from any quarter in the hope of keeping the ministry afloat. He showed a greater willingness for self-sacrifice than he had exhibited even when writing to Gladstone a year previously. Before the elections were over he asked Palmerston for his aid, offering him his own position as Leader of the Commons in the hope that he would bring a sizeable number of supporters over to the government side. But Palmerston refused, saying on 3 May that for 'many reasons' such an arrangement was impossible.[47] Palmerston no doubt believed that, as the Italian war of independence had broken out on 29 April, he would soon be able to form another ministry with the extensive pro-Italian popular support. Derby approached Gladstone, and was again rebuffed. Even more ardent for Italian independence than Palmerston, Gladstone preferred to end his anomalous situation in a different way by aligning with the Liberal leader. Italy provided his sole official reason. Disraeli tried to win more support in Ireland by urging the appointment of more Catholics in the Dublin administration. He also hinted to radicals that he might advocate a much wider Reform measure than the recent bill – an interesting foreshadowing of his wide acceptance of radical amendments to his bill of 1867.

After the elections it seemed that the ministry would soon have to go out. More than domestic issues, Italian independence had dominated the contests, and support for it was growing.[48] Palmerston and Russell were hailed as champions of independence, while Derby was unfairly depicted as a supporter of Austria. The Liberals continued to become more unified after the election, and were soon to grow in number through the accession of the remaining Peelites. At an important party meeting at Willis's Rooms on 6 June, Palmerston and Russell each agreed to serve under the other if either was invited to form a ministry.[49] It was also decided at the meeting that the twenty-five year old

Marquess of Hartington would move a vote of no confidence in the Government in the debate on the Address. Union of political individuals and groups was proceeding, helping, at the end of the fractious fifties, to restore the two-party system of twenty years before. But this was a movement that benefited only the Liberals and did not assist the beleaguered Conservatives.

The day before the division on Hartington's motion, Disraeli acted on an impulse which resembled his sudden interview with Bright in December 1852, when it had seemed that the previous Conservative ministry was about to be overturned. In a last-minute throw to save the Government he suggested to Derby that they should both retire from their positions of leadership and give the sole lead to Stanley. On account of the latter's enthusiasm for progress it was possible that he could attract support from Liberals, and perhaps commence a re-structuring of politics which would benefit Conservative party interests. But the suggestion obtained no favour from Derby. On 11 June, despite a fighting speech by Disraeli, the Government was beaten on Hartington's motion by 323 to 310. Derby immediately resigned, and the Queen reluctantly re-appointed Palmerston as premier. Gladstone, despite having supported Derby's ministry in the division, agreed to take office under Palmerston. The other remaining Peelites also gave their support to the new Government. Politics were assuming a more stable appearance than they had done since 1846, but it was a stability which favoured the Liberals and not the party of Disraeli.

. . .

OPPOSITION, 1859–65

The next six years were particularly discouraging to Disraeli's quest for power. Not only had the Liberals been returned again with a majority large enough to keep them in office for several years, but Palmerston, as the champion of the *status quo* at home and of British power abroad, appealed generally to Conservatives. The new Government obtained much more respect from Conservatives than the Aberdeen Coalition had done, and so Disraeli's means of opposing it were limited. He was therefore more willing than before to follow Derby's attitude of patiently biding his time.

But a man of Disraeli's usually persistent activity would have found it impossible to forego all chances of exploiting cracks in his opponents' ranks. The Liberals were more united than they had been earlier in the 1850s. Russell and Palmerston had buried their hatchet, and the former took office under the latter. Although there was a good deal of radical activity, especially from 'political Dissenters' and trade unionists, there was for a few more years less strenuous nation-wide campaigning in general than in the later 1830s and the 1840s. But there were still sizeable weaknesses in the Liberal defences. Roman Catholics found some Liberal policies uncomfortable. They remembered the Ecclesiastical Titles Act, and were affronted by Palmerston's support for the Italian unification movement with its implied rejection of the Pope's temporal power. Nonconformists, moreover, were still wanting relief from most of the disabilities they had been contending against since the early 1830s. In particular, they were campaigning hard to obtain the abolition of church rates, which were levied in order to maintain the parish churches. Palmerston's Government was not very ready to listen to their demands, but since it needed their electoral support it was also unwilling to give an exclusive commitment to the defence of Established Church privilege.

Basically, Disraeli was willing to try to gain support even from Nonconformists, as he was to show later. But his party allegiance and support committed him to defend the Established Churches to a large extent; and although the Whigs were also so committed, they were in a dilemma because of their unwillingness to alienate their Nonconformist following. There was therefore an opportunity, which Disraeli seized, to appear in the guise of Established Church champion, especially over the issue of church rates. This posture – and it was little more than a posture, for it was virtually abandoned, where church rates were concerned, in the later 1860s – helped him to build up distinctive Conservative morale against the seemingly impregnable Palmerston. Stanley, however, who wanted to settle the church rate issue by compromise, can hardly have approved of his stand, and even Derby became rather alarmed.[50]

The stand on the Church helped to strengthen Disraeli amidst trouble he was having over his position in the Conservative party and in his personal life. In personal matters, money was still a nagging if very familiar worry. Disraeli's debts continued to increase. In 1857 the Duke of Portland, Lord George Bentinck's elder brother, who entertained Peelite views, demanded repayment of his share of the loan made by the Bentincks for the purchase of Hughenden Manor. Disraeli had to borrow the required amount from money-lenders, who charged a high rate of interest, and his total indebtedness approached £60,000. Before long, however, the situation began to improve, justifying Disraeli's Micawberish financial attitude that one had only to wait for something to turn up. In 1859 he obtained a government pension of £2,000 a year which became due to him after his second term as Chancellor of the Exchequer. Another fortunate stroke came at the end of 1862. A wealthy political supporter, Andrew Montagu (a large landowner in Yorkshire, and a bachelor) offered to do his bit financially for the party. It was suggested that he might reduce Disraeli's debts. Accordingly, he offered to pay off these debts, charging Disraeli interest of only three per cent p.a. (far less than the money-lenders), in return for a mortgage on Hughenden. Disraeli naturally accepted, and reckoned that he saved at least £4,200 a year through this generous transaction. Then there occurred, in September 1863, the death of one of Disraeli's intimate correspondents, Mrs Brydges Willyams of Torquay. This rich and very old widow (according to Stanley's diary she was ninety-four), a Christianised Jew like Disraeli and an ardent admirer of him, left him over £30,000 in her will 'in testimony of my affection, and in approbation and admiration of his efforts to vindicate the race of Israel'. Through these windfalls Disraeli was at last in financial balance. One who had been twice Chancellor of the Exchequer had become personally solvent.

Disraeli was too used to debt, and too used to taking it in his stride, for this improved state of security to have done much to increase his high level of political commitment. It might even have had the reverse effect, for it was complained that he was becoming apathetic towards public affairs in the years from 1863 to 1865. His better financial condition, however, did reveal itself in the amounts of money he proceeded to spend on beautifying and enlarging his estate, and on improving the cottages of his tenantry.

A problem for Disraeli in this period was scarcely less familiar than debt – the uncertainty of his position as a Conservative leader. At the time this arose from rumblings of discontent among the 'ultras' (or firm right-wingers) in the party, such as George Bentinck (MP for West Norfolk), Lord Robert Cecil, Sir Rainald Knightley and Charles Newdegate. The 1859 Reform Bill left a good deal of bitterness among such as these. Lord Robert Cecil (later Lord Cranborne and Marquess of Salisbury) attacked Disraeli and his Reform Bill in an anonymous article in the *Quarterly Review* of April 1860. The bill, said the article, was:

> ... of a piece with a policy which had long misguided and discredited the Conservative party in the House of Commons. To crush the Whigs by combining with the Radicals was the first and last maxim of Mr Disraeli's Parliamentary tactics ... he had been a successful leader to this extent, that he had made any Government while he was in Opposition next to an impossibility. His tactics were so various, so flexible, so shameless – the net by which his combinations were gathered in was so wide – he had so admirable a knack of enticing into the same lobby a happy family of proud old Tories and foaming Radicals, martial squires jealous of their country's honour, and manufacturers who had written it off their books as an unmarketable commodity – that so long as his party backed him no Government was strong enough to hold out against his attacks.[51]

This was superb journalistic knockabout, but it considerably exaggerated Disraeli's manoeuvres and the extent of their success in the 1850s. At the time this article appeared, Disraeli was arguably trying to rid himself of such imputations by appearing as a Church defence champion. The view he had assumed at this time was that the privileges of the Church of England should be fully vindicated; while Gladstone was soon to take the opposite view that the best way to defend that Church was to abandon many of its privileges. Disraeli's most distinctive contribution to the politics of the early 1860s was to oppose the Dissenting campaign against church rates, although the lack of any permanency in this attitude was shown both by his acquiescence in a settlement of the dispute in 1868 and by his having favoured a compromise solution in 1853 and 1859.[52]

In 1860 Disraeli began to oppose successive annual bills for the abolition of church rates. In 1859 the bill had obtained a majority of seventy on its second reading in the Commons, but in 1860 the majority in the Lower House on this reading dropped to only twenty-nine. On both occasions the Lords rejected the bill by a large majority. In 1861 there was a tie in the Commons on the third reading, 274 votes being given on each side, and the Speaker cast his deciding vote against the bill. In the following year the bill was defeated in the Commons by one vote on the second reading, and in 1863 by ten votes. The hopes of the campaigners had been rolled back, and Disraeli shared the feeling of success in their defeat. He had spoken repeatedly in the Commons against the bills, and when Derby suggested that his uncompromising stand might be politically unwise he replied that he thought it a promising means of boosting Conservative support.[53]

With the same object in view he also helped to defeat bills to remove the Nonconformist grievance over burials. He spoke at meetings of clergymen in Buckinghamshire in defence of the establishment principle, the remaining privileges of the Church, and the need to increase Church funds and Church members.[54] He even aligned himself with the traditionalists in the current controversy over Darwinism. At a celebrated meeting at Oxford in November 1864 he assured Bishop Samuel Wilberforce that, in reply to the question 'Is man an ape or an angel?', he would say: 'I am on the side of the angels'.[55] Given his speculative mind, however, it may be hazarded that he was unlikely to be any more consistent in this opinion than he was in his ecclesiastical policy.

His few years as a leading Church defender were typical of Disraeli's politics. He would take advantage of whatever opportunities were offered to him by his antagonists (in this case Palmerston's Government) through their own political commitments or their indecisiveness. Among the Liberals, Nonconformists were calling for change. However, the Whigs, although differing in their views, were wary of conceding much to them because the cry for disestablishment might gather momentum and cause serious divisions in the Liberal party. On the other hand, because of their Nonconformist alliance (shaky though it was) the Whigs did not appear very reliable Church defenders, so Disraeli stepped forward with characteristic aplomb to fill the bill. The episode made no permanent encroachment on his more usual adjustment to the liberal tendencies of the age – any more than did his parallel opposition to Liberal Parliamentary Reform proposals in 1860 and 1865. Reforms were only to be opposed when it seemed that there was party advantage in the resistance, just as they were to be adopted when it seemed there would be advantage in that approach.

Parliamentary Reform revived as an enthusiastic cause in the country in the early and mid 1860s, and by 1865 there was growing public pressure on Parliament to pass a moderate Reform Bill. Disraeli had attacked the Government effectively in 1864. His attacks had included the introduction of a censure motion against it for not defending Denmark in the war over Schleswig-Holstein, and this motion was lost by only eighteen votes.[56] But there was another disappointing general election for the Conservatives in July 1865, when Palmerston vindicated his lasting popularity by obtaining a majority of sixty, twenty more than in 1859. The results in Scotland and London, Disraeli lamented in a letter to Derby, were particularly gloomy for the Conservatives. He might have added that the Welsh results were no brighter, for the Conservatives lost the majority they had had in Wales since 1835. In Ireland they did relatively well, and in England they slightly increased their total. But over the United Kingdom as a whole their seats went down by eight.[57] 'Unless the basis be extended', wrote Disraeli in yet another allusion to the perennial need to obtain more voting strength, a Conservative majority would never be won.[58] He was no doubt referring to the desirability of introducing a further Reform Bill if another minority Conservative Government took office. This did indeed occur, sooner than he probably imagined.

The rather dull surface of British politics after the Palmerstonian electoral victory was suddenly broken by the premier's death on 18 October 1865. The view among politicians was that the pent-up demand for Reform would have to receive some relief, and they expressed jubilation or apprehension at the prospect, depending on their attitude to the question. Lord Shaftesbury wrote despondently about the departure of the late premier, his brother-in-law: 'Thus goes the "Ultimus Romanorum", and now begins ... the greatest social, political and religious revolution that England has yet endured. What an instrument he has been in the hands of God the Almighty.' But John Bright, from an opposite political viewpoint, wrote that Palmerston had 'stood for some years between "the old and the new", and his removal will make a real and probably not a small revolution'.[59] Whether one were joyful or otherwise at the prospect, a new era of reform was about to begin.

Disraeli was elated by the vistas opened up by Palmerston's demise. Stanley, visiting him at Hughenden, found his spirits lifted and his confidence boosted after the disappointment of the summer election. It seemed, Stanley wrote, as if 'the prospect of renewed political life had excited him afresh, and that he had thrown off the lethargy which has been growing upon him for the last year or two'.[60] But renewed political possibilities by no means signalled the end of Disraeli's lengthy uphill struggle since the fall of Peel. The Liberals still had a majority, indeed a recently increased one. It was the new Liberal Government, with Earl Russell (the former Lord John) as the Prime Minister, which would decide what measures of reform to introduce.

Disraeli's uncertain political position continued for another eight years. But within nine months of Palmerston's death he and his colleagues formed a ministry once again and planned reforming legislation. This was only another brief minority Government, but it was the longest of the three since 1846 and it did succeed in enacting a major bill of domestic reform. During the fourteen years between 1866 and 1880 Disraeli came to play a much bigger and more constructive part in politics and greatly consolidated his power.

.   .   .

NOTES

1. Quoted in R. Blake, *Disraeli*, London 1966, p. 259.
2. W.F. Monypenny and G.E. Buckle, *The Life of Benjamin Disraeli, Earl of Beaconsfield*, 6 vols, London 1910–20, vol. III (1846–55), pp. 121–4 (hereafter cited as Mony-penny & Buckle).

3. Ibid., pp. 124–6.
4. Sarah Bradford, *Disraeli*, London 1982, pp. 194–5; Edward Stanley's diary, 20 March 1849, in J. Vincent (ed.), *Disraeli, Derby and the Conservative Party: journals and memoirs of Edward Henry, Lord Stanley, 1849–69*, Hassocks 1978, pp. 1–2; R. Stewart, *The Politics of Protection: Lord Derby and the Protectionist Party, 1841–52*, Cambridge 1971, pp. 134–8.
5. Monypenny & Buckle, vol. III, p. 140.
6. Ibid., p. 312; Blake, *Disraeli*, pp. 309–10.
7. R.W. Davis, *Disraeli*, London 1976, pp. 79, 100; Monypenny & Buckle, vol. III, pp. 196–7, 213–33.
8. Blake, *Disraeli*, p. 291.
9. Davis, *Disraeli*, pp. 110–11.
10. Ibid., pp. 105–6.
11. G.I.T. Machin, *Politics and the Churches in Great Britain, 1832 to 1868*, Oxford 1977, pp. 223–4.
12. Monypenny & Buckle, vol. III, pp. 286–96; Blake, *Disraeli*, pp. 301–5; Davis, *Disraeli*, pp. 107–8; Stewart, *The Politics of Protection*, pp. 183–4.
13. Davis, *Disraeli*, pp. 108–10.
14. Quoted in Blake, *Disraeli*, p. 311.
15. Bradford, *Disraeli*, pp. 219–20.
16. Blake, *Disraeli*, p. 311.
17. Machin, *Politics and the Churches, 1832 to 1868*, pp. 229–33.
18. Monypenny & Buckle, vol. III, pp. 407–22.
19. 7 August 1852; Vincent, *Disraeli, Derby and the Conservative Party*, p. 79. Cf. Monypenny & Buckle, vol. III, pp. 426–49; and (for quite a favourable recent view of the budget) P.R. Ghosh, 'Disraelian Conservatism: a financial approach', *English Historical Review*, vol. XCIX (1984), pp. 269–82.
20. *Hansard's Parliamentary Debates*, third series, vol. CXXIII, cols 836–907; Vincent, *Disraeli, Derby and the Conservative Party*, p. 86.
21. Monypenny & Buckle, vol. III, pp. 438–9. For this interview see also R.A.J. Walling (ed.), *The Diaries of John Bright*, London 1930, pp. 128–30.
22. Monypenny & Buckle, vol. III, p. 441; Stewart, *The Politics of Protection*, p. 213.
23. Quoted in Bradford, *Disraeli*, p. 212. Cf. Stanley's diary,

16 December 1852; Vincent, *Disraeli, Derby and the Conservative Party*, p. 89.

24. Monypenny & Buckle, vol. III, pp. 476–80.
25. Vincent, *Disraeli, Derby and the Conservative Party*, pp. 95–6, 104, 114, 135.
26. Blake, *Disraeli*, p. 396.
27. Monypenny & Buckle, vol. III, pp. 359, 483, 500–1.
28. Ibid., pp. 489–506; Vincent, *Disraeli, Derby and the Conservative Party*, p. 102.
29. Quoted in Monypenny & Buckle, vol. III, p. 521.
30. Blake, *Disraeli*, pp. 354–5; J.B. Conacher, *The Aberdeen Coalition, 1852–5*, Cambridge 1968, p. 122.
31. Vincent, *Disraeli, Derby and the Conservative Party*, p. 96.
32. Davis, *Disraeli*, p. 121; Monypenny & Buckle, vol. III, pp. 511–12.
33. Monypenny & Buckle, vol. III, p. 483.
34. Ibid., p. 528.
35. Quoted in Blake, *Disraeli*, p. 419.
36. Quoted in ibid., p. 360.
37. Vincent, *Disraeli, Derby and the Conservative Party*, pp. 130–1.
38. Quoted in Blake, *Disraeli*, p. 363.
39. Monypenny & Buckle, vol. IV, p. 21, Cf. A. Hawkins, *Parliament, Party and the Art of Politics in Britain, 1855–9*, London 1987, pp. 46–7.
40. Quoted in Blake, *Disraeli*, p. 368.
41. Bradford, *Disraeli*, pp. 232–4.
42. Disraeli to Mrs Brydges Willyams, 13 April 1857; quoted in Blake, *Disraeli*, p. 375.
43. Ibid., pp. 375–7.
44. Monypenny & Buckle, vol. IV, pp. 157–9.
45. Davis, *Disraeli*, pp. 133–5; Blake, *Disraeli*, pp. 399–400; Hawkins, *Parliament, Party, and the Art of Politics*, pp. 177–225.
46. *McCalmont's Parliamentary Poll Book: British election results, 1832–1918* (ed. J. Vincent and M. Stenton, Brighton 1971), p. 332b.
47. Monypenny & Buckle, vol. IV, pp. 235–7.
48. C.T. McIntire, *England against the Papacy, 1858–61: Tories, Liberals and the overthrow of papal temporal power during the Italian Risorgimento*, Cambridge 1983, pp. 109–11.
49. D. Southgate, *The Passing of the Whigs, 1832–86*, London 1962, pp. 290–5.

50. Machin, *Politics and the Churches, 1832 to 1868*, p. 317.
51. Quoted in Davis, *Disraeli*, p. 139. On the discontent of some Conservatives with Disraeli in the early 1860s, see Vincent, *Disraeli, Derby and the Conservative Party*, pp. 197, 202, 204, 208.
52. Conacher, *The Aberdeen Coalition*, p. 107; Davis, *Disraeli*, pp. 140, 142; Monypenny & Buckle, vol. IV, p. 354.
53. Letters quoted in Machin, *Politics and the Churches, 1832 to 1868,* pp. 317–18. See Monypenny & Buckle, vol. IV, p. 354ff.
54. Machin, *Politics and the Churches, 1832 to 1868*, p. 317.
55. Davis, *Disraeli*, pp. 143–4.
56. Monypenny & Buckle, vol. IV, pp. 345–7, 404–5.
57. *McCalmont's Parliamentary Poll Book*, p. 332b.
58. Monypenny & Buckle, vol. IV, p. 416.
59. Quoted in Machin, *Politics and the Churches, 1832 to 1868*, p. 334.
60. Vincent, *Disraeli, Derby and the Conservative Party*, p. 237.

Chapter 5

STRUGGLE WITH GLADSTONE, 1865–1874

. . .

PARLIAMENTARY TRIUMPH AND ELECTORAL FAILURE, 1865–8

The next period in Disraeli's life banished any apathy he might recently have felt. Palmerston's death brought the Liberal and Conservative leaders into sharper conflict with each other over issues of reform. The late premier had pursued policies of defending British interests abroad and general quiescence at home which gained wide Conservative support. He was succeeded as Prime Minister by Earl Russell, and as Liberal leader in the Commons by Gladstone, and both of these were more enthusiastic for domestic reform than Palmerston had been. Russell was far more anxious than Palmerston to carry a Parliamentary Reform Bill, while Gladstone had recently clashed with Palmerston over his new-found reforming enthusiasms, including Parliamentary Reform, support for Nonconformist claims for relief, and encouragement of the reform demands of Irish Catholics.

None of this developing interest in reform on Gladstone's part differed fundamentally from opinions held by Disraeli. The latter had long advocated Parliamentary Reform and, through his effort of 1859, had become prominent among its votaries. He represented the desire for Parliamentary Reform in the Conservative interest, however, while Russell and now Gladstone expressed the rival desire for it in the Liberal interest. The contending desires would be expressed, as they had been previously, by markedly different electoral proposals. It is true that Disraeli's recent public attitude of defending Church privilege and rebutting Dissenting claims seemed to differ strongly from Gladstone's subtler developing tendency to advocate concessions to Nonconformists as a means of Church defence. But Disraeli also was prepared to make concessions to both Nonconformists and Catholics, and in the next Conservative ministry he showed a face more yielding than the rigid one he had recently shown in Opposition. To a considerable extent the policies of Disraeli and Gladstone were coming to rival each other on account of their similarities rather than their differences. The two up-and-coming leaders clashed fiercely, but over the detail of policy and differences of approach rather than over any fundamental disjunction of principle.

The three years between the end of Palmerston's second Government and the beginning of Gladstone's first ministry gave Disraeli a lot more political excitement and promise than he had experienced since 1846. In this period he greatly increased his fame and reputation, and became both leader of his party and Prime Minister for the first time. But, for all his effort and success, the consummation of political power in Britain – a parliamentary majority – still eluded him. By the end of 1868 the exciting and tantalising phase had come to an end. Gladstone obtained the majority and took the premiership. Disraeli was again consigned to Opposition and had to meet some quite serious internal criticisms of his leadership, until in 1874 he finally reached his apogee when a majority at last was his.

As the Liberals retained, in the years from 1865 to 1874, the dominance they had usually possessed in the Commons since 1846, Disraeli had to continue trying to divide and weaken the Liberal forces. He did so with a good deal more success than hitherto, attaining by this means the passage of a Parliamentary Reform Bill in 1867. It was clear that Russell and Gladstone would introduce a Reform Bill in the session of 1866, but it seemed likely that there would be some Liberal opposition to it. Robert Lowe, a Liberal MP and former junior minister, was anxious to stop the country falling into anything so dangerous as democracy. Together with some party colleagues he had supported the Conservatives in rejecting a private member's Borough Franchise Bill in 1865.[1] The prospect was opening for Disraeli of resuming his tactics of dividing one Liberal section from another and using the Liberal opposition to Reform to defeat a Liberal bill on the subject. Conservative interests lay in siding with Liberal opponents of even a moderate measure in order to defeat Russell's Government.

These tactics succeeded triumphantly in 1866. The ministerial Reform Bill, introduced in the Commons by Gladstone on 12 March, alarmed Conservatives by proposing to alter the electorates in county constituencies in ways which threatened to weaken the Conservative hold on those areas. Lowe headed a group of about forty supporters, consisting mostly of aristocratic Whigs, who also opposed these proposals because of their anti-paternalist nature. Owing to the minute Old Testament knowledge of John Bright, which as an ardent reformer he scornfully applied to these malcontents, they became immortalised as the 'Adullamite' cave. If most of the Adullamites voted with the Conservatives, the combination would be numerous enough to defeat the ministry. Disraeli would scarcely have obtained the support of many of the Adullamites for an immediate head-on challenge to the Government. Instead, he won their support gradually by piecemeal attempts to reduce the enfranchisement proposals in both counties and boroughs. Amendments to the bill obtained larger and larger numbers of votes during June until, on the eighteenth, the Government lost by 315 votes to 304 on an amendment to the borough franchise moved by an Adullamite.[2]

After several days of uncertainty, Russell resigned on 26 June. During the brief period since the ministry's defeat the Adullamites had been pressing their interest in a coalition with the Conservatives. But Derby did not respond to their approaches. He complied instead with Disraeli's urgent advice in a letter of 25 June: 'The question is not Adullamite; it is national. You *must* take the Government; the honour of your house and the necessity of the country alike require it.'[3] It was obviously in Disraeli's interest that his own position should not be threatened by the entry of Adullamites into a coalition ministry. That Derby should 'take the Government' was also the unanimous opinion of twenty-two leading Conservatives whom Derby called together on 28 June, the day after the Queen had invited him to form a ministry. It was the view of all except one of these that he should form a purely Conservative ministry if the Adullamites would not join. Derby in fact gave very little opportunity to the Adullamites, and his new Government was almost purely Conservative, only one Liberal joining it. Disraeli's position as second in command and Leader of the House of Commons, which might well have had to be sacrificed if a coalition had occurred, was secure for yet another spell of minority government.[4]

The new Cabinet was stronger than the two previous Conservative ones. The third Derby ministry scored more highly than its predecessors in passing a variety of important legislation and obtaining a spectacular success in carrying a major Parliamentary Reform Bill. The question of parliamentary reform had come more prominently and widely before the country than at any time since 1832. Agitation for it had commenced about two years before. Popular demand for a new Act was encouraged by the Liberal bill of 1866 and continued after the bill's defeat on 18 June. From 23 to 25 July occurred the invasion and occupation of London's Hyde Park by a crowd. This seems to have helped to direct the new ministers' minds towards the idea of evolving another Conservative Reform Bill. Disraeli wrote to Derby on 29 July that the new ministry might adopt the Liberal bill in a modified and extended form. The suggested extension lay in his proposal to give more seats to industrial boroughs, thus introducing a redistribution of seats which the Liberal bill had lacked. Disraeli believed that such proposals would be easily carried in the current House of Commons, and would bring the Conservatives advantage over their rivals.[5]

But neither popular vociferousness nor ministerial interest in the issue lasted. During the parliamentary recess, memories of the Hyde Park riots faded and Disraeli's concern with Reform receded at the same time. From mid-September, however, Derby, urged on by Queen Victoria, began to stress that it would be advisable to deal with Reform. Derby proposed that resolutions should be introduced in Parliament in 1867 but that legislation should be postponed until 1868, and Disraeli appreciated the skill of this tactic as a means of trying to ensure that the Conservatives would have a reasonable spell in office.[6] But Derby did not succeed in reviving his lieutenant's recent enthusiasm for Reform until the end of the year. On 3 January 1867 Disraeli wrote to his chief that the matter must be addressed. This was after Derby had made a crucial suggestion to him on 22 December: 'of all possible hares to start, I do not know a better than the extension to household suffrage, coupled with plurality of voting'.[7] Thus the central feature of the 1867 Reform Act, household suffrage in the boroughs, originated with Derby.

On 11 February 1867 Disraeli introduced the Cabinet's resolutions in the Commons. But on the following day, when it was clear that mere resolutions would not have a favourable reception, Disraeli suddenly announced that ministers would bring in a bill on 25 February. He probably wanted to thwart the introduction of a bill by the Liberals. But he had acted without the authority of the Cabinet. Conservative ministers who did not favour a Reform policy became very suspicious of him and began to contemplate resignation from the Government. To the consternation of these ministers, it was decided in Cabinet that the bill would propose a male ratepayers' franchise in the boroughs, and plural voting (to a maximum of two votes) which would be based on 'fancy franchises' such as a professional qualification and a certain amount of money held in a deposit account. The ratepaying franchise would not be restricted by any financial limit, but by the provision that only personal ratepayers could vote, not those who 'compounded' to pay their rates at a discount through their landlord.

There followed something like a panic among ministers. On 24 February Viscount Cranborne, the Earl of Carnarvon and General Jonathan Peel (brother of the late premier) said they would resign on account of the extensive enfranchisement likely to occur. In order to try to prevent these resignations the Cabinet decided on 25 February, just over two hours before its proposals were to be announced in the Commons, to introduce a more restricted bill – a household franchise of £6 in the boroughs and £20 in the counties, together with fancy franchises.

This sudden 'ten minute bill', which was unsatisfactory to ministers of all shades of opinion on the question, received its name because it was agreed on only that length of time before a party meeting arranged for 2.30 p.m. Two hours after that, Disraeli had to announce the details of the 'ten minute bill' in the Commons. He found it was more unpopular there than it was even in the Cabinet. Many Conservative backbenchers had had their appetites whetted for a wide measure introduced by their own party. Their hopes were deflated by the 'ten minute bill', and they tried to revive the original promise of a broad measure by pressing for the adoption of male household suffrage. A large majority of 150 Conservative MPs, meeting at the Carlton Club on 28 February, expressed dislike of the 'ten minute bill' and favoured household suffrage with accompanying safeguards of three years' residence, personal payment of rates, and plural voting. Disraeli was delighted when the Adullamites also took up household suffrage with plurality, because this revealed the continuance of Liberal divisions. If household suffrage was dividing the Conservatives, it was also dividing the Liberals, and Disraeli could take what was now his traditional course of exploiting the latter divisions in order to strengthen his own party.[8]

On 2 March the Cabinet went back on its tracks. It now decided to drop the 'ten minute bill' and re-adopt its wider measure, proposing a manhood personal ratepaying franchise with plurality of voting. Cranborne, Carnarvon and Peel could not stomach such a measure, on the reasonable grounds that it might wreck well-established Conservative influence in many constituencies and only aid the Liberals. So they resigned. To try to prevent further defections Derby and Disraeli held a party meeting on 15 March to explain their bill. This action, Lord Blake has said, was 'a great success. It made members feel that they were being kept in the picture, that their advice was appreciated and that their leaders trusted them. If Peel had pursued the same course over the Corn Laws he might have fared better.'[9] Three days later the bill was presented to the Commons. During the ensuing period of intense parliamentary excitement the convolutions which had already occurred were continued and magnified. Disraeli attained well-deserved parliamentary triumph and party acclaim.

It is well known how the widened measure introduced on 18 March became much wider still before it passed. During this time Disraeli's unrivalled ability to grasp political opportunity and his sparkling oratory enlivened the proceedings and kept the Liberal majority in disarray. In the debates he rose to a height of parliamentary performance he had not displayed since 1846. His old friend James Clay, a Liberal MP, believed (as he told his colleagues, no doubt from his knowledge of Disraeli) that the most effective way of widening the suffrage was to vote for the Conservative bill on its second reading, and then move amendments which a grateful Disraeli would accept in order to confound Gladstone and get his bill through. Gladstone failed both to defeat the second reading and to carry subsequent amendments against radical and Adullamite opposition. Radical amendments, on the other hand, to reduce the two years' residence requirement to one year, to enfranchise lodgers, and to abolish compounding for payment of rates (which would have the effect of enfranchising about half a million people), were accepted by Disraeli and carried. But there was so much objection to the abolition of compounding (on account of its financial benefits) that it was allowed to continue, at the expense of franchise extension in time for the general election of 1868. It was not until an Act of 1869 had simply enfranchised compounders that these potential electors were able to get on to the register.

The successful radical amendments seemed to make the fancy franchises superfluous, and they were dropped from the bill. The county franchise, unlike the borough franchise, was not opened to adult male householders, but the property requirement was much reduced. A pioneering motion for women's suffrage by John Stuart Mill failed by 196 votes to 73, but commenced frequent parliamentary consideration of this claim until it succeeded fifty-one years later.

The Reform Bill for England and Wales became law in August 1867. Similar bills for Scotland and Ireland, a Registration of Voters Bill, a Boundary Bill and a Corrupt Practices Bill went through Parliament in 1868. The number enfranchised by the bills was the largest in any nineteenth-century measure. Despite this, democracy was only slightly advanced, and its votaries were left wanting a great deal more. From the Government's viewpoint there had to be restrictions on the extension lest the bill simply enfranchised more Nonconformists and trade unionists who would vote for the Liberals as seeming more likely to favour their claims. There was no point in Disraeli's gaining a great parliamentary triumph and new prestige among his fellow-Conservatives if the result was simply to give the Liberals a larger majority. So Disraeli introduced and carried a Redistribution Bill in 1867 which transferred a total of only fifty-two seats, about half to the counties and only nine to the large cities where most of the new electors resided. This was the smallest transfer of seats in any of the three Reform measures in the nineteenth century; it was considered by its authors to be a necessary antidote to the largest creation of votes in the nineteenth century if the Conservatives were to get a majority.

Further evidence that party interest rather than principle was behind the Reform can be found in the establishment of a government Boundary Commission filled with Conservative landowners. This transferred suburb-dwelling county voters to borough seats in order to keep the counties rural and (it was hoped) Conservative, and to make the towns less Liberal. Even though the initial proposals were watered down by a parliamentary Select Committee (which Disraeli opposed) in 1868, 700,000 people were transferred by this method.[10]

The Reform measures of 1867 and 1868 were undoubtedly the biggest achievement of the Government. Along with it, however, though quite independent of it, went constructive legislation in social reform and a successful intervention in overseas affairs. The ministry's social reform record in 1867 was significant, as Paul Smith has noted.[11] This collection of reforms extended State intervention, illustrating how the latter was gradually, if not yet very markedly, encroaching on *laissez-faire*. A Factory Acts Extension Act and an Hours of Labour Regulation Bill enlarged the scope of the existing factory legislation, to the benefit of one and a half million women and children. A Merchant Shipping Act, intended to be the prelude to a larger measure, provided a system of government inspection of vessels. Another Act made the Poor Law Board a permanent body. An important Public Health Act, taken over from Russell's ministry, had been passed in 1866, and was followed by a similar Public Health (Scotland) Act the next year. These two Acts were the first effective measures of State compulsion in this field: as has been said, they 'not only gave health authorities powers but prescribed for them duties, and provided for their coercion where they defaulted'.[12] The original Liberal bill had given powers of compulsion to local authorities but the Conservative Government shifted them to the Home Secretary, thereby significantly enlarging the power of central government over the localities. Several other measures of social amelioration were also passed, including a Master and Servant Bill (piloted by a private member) which removed the penalty of imprisonment for breach of contract by an employee.

Success, not only over franchise extension and social reform but also over a neo-Palmerstonian imperial venture, accrued to this Government. In November 1867 a military expedition was despatched from India against King Theodore of Abyssinia, to compel him to release the British envoys and other British citizens he had incarcerated. News came in April 1868 of the complete (though financially costly) success of the operation, Theodore having killed himself and no new imperial annexation having taken place.[13] The episode was an isolated one, and cannot convincingly be seen as the start of Disraelian absorption in overseas affairs; though Disraeli may have seen it in retrospect as a harbinger of his important trend in this direction, which began in 1872. He was certainly delighted with the outcome of the Abyssinian venture, seeing it no doubt as the kind of operation he had secretly admired when undertaken by Palmerston. Now, such a venture had been successfully carried through by his own Government. Moreover, he was interested in constitutional imperial consolidation as well as the military vindication of imperial might, and the former kind of imperial development was exemplified in 1867 by the establishment of Canadian federation, though Disraeli was not directly involved in this achievement.

Indeed, the ministry of 1866–8 was the one period of Disraeli's life when his three main lines of innovative policy – Parliamentary Reform, social amelioration, and imperial vindication and consolidation – came together at the same time. Even the social reforms and overseas successes of 1874–8 could not repeat this level of concentration, as further Parliamentary Reform had at that time no part in Disraeli's schemes. In 1867–8, moreover, the three lines of policy paralleled each other in their clear success. The Government of 1866–8, despite its minority status and its ultimate election defeat, can be counted as outstandingly successful, helping to counteract the failures of the two previous Conservative ministries. The Government of 1852 was known mainly for its failed budget, that of 1858–9 mainly for its failed Reform Bill, but the ministry of 1866–8 scintillated with victory in electoral, social and imperial fields.

Though still without the full power of a majority, Disraeli managed to achieve a great deal at this time. His successes made his eventual heavy defeat at the polls all the more galling.

Most Conservatives were delighted with the Parliamentary Reform triumph of 1867, and with the man who had achieved it. Disraeli gained, if only temporarily, a popularity with his party which was greater than ever before. Only Cranborne and a handful of allies ('the Cranborne Cave') turned their backs disgustedly on the applause and accused him of betraying party principles. But the triumph was quite short-lived. Gladstone, who had lost badly in 1867, regained the initiative in 1868 and won a much enlarged Liberal majority at the end of that year.

Early in 1868 Disraeli achieved another glowing political success, that of gaining the premiership. He was appointed Prime Minister at the end of February, succeeding Derby whose gout had got the better of him, causing him first to resign and later (in October 1869) to die. Disraeli shared not only Conservatism but gout with Derby, and ironically Disraeli was attacked by gout himself early in 1868. But he recovered, and was soon cock-a-hoop at topping 'the greasy poll' – as he characteristically referred to his having attained his life's ambition. Despite his elation on receiving Derby's crucial letter asking him if he was ready to take over, he had sufficient command of himself to reply on 20 February in the following terms to his senior colleague of so many years:

> I have not sufficient command of myself at this moment to express what I feel about what has happened . . . so rapidly and so unexpectedly. All I will say is that I never contemplated nor desired it. I was entirely content with my position, and all I aspired to was that, after a Government of tolerable length, and at least fair repute, my retirement from public affairs should have accompanied your own; satisfied that I had enjoyed my opportunity in life, and proud that I had been long confidentially connected with one of the most eminent men of my time, and for whom I entertain profound respect and affection.[14]

Disraeli's appointment by a very welcoming Queen, announced by Stanley in the Commons on 25 February, followed three uncertain days between the time, on 21 February, when Derby wrote to Queen Victoria saying he intended to resign and advising her to appoint Disraeli, and 24 February when the latter received a message of invitation to form a ministry.[15] There was nothing more sinister in this delay than Derby's wishing to see the Queen in order to hand over the seals in person and to make recommendations for peerages.[16] But the temporary uncertainty, and the fact that Derby took it on himself to recommend Disraeli to the Queen, has led to the suggestion that Disraeli was not an assured successor to the premiership, and that it needed private concert between Derby and the Queen to 'smuggle him privily' into it.[17] There is nothing to suggest, however, that Disraeli's succession was resisted in any way, even by those Conservatives who obviously did not like it. He was the natural and unrivalled successor, not least because of his triumph of 1867 which was acclaimed by most of his party. Stanley, who would have been the only really credible rival, repeatedly said he did not want to take the lead; indeed, he directly assisted Disraeli to take it at this juncture.[18] Cranborne, very able though he was, represented only a small, disaffected group in the party which had little influence on the majority of Conservatives. In February 1868 Disraeli still stood on a peak of success after the events of 1867, and he reaped the reward of his current popularity by enjoying a smooth and unchallenged accession to the premiership.

In forming his first Cabinet – an operation causing some upset because of one ex-minister's disappointed hope – Disraeli asked Cranborne to join. But the latter refused. The offer was well-intentioned, but it was far too early to make it, and it was not until 1874 that Cranborne, even then with considerable reluctance, buried the hatchet with Disraeli. Although it did not have unanimous Conservative support, however, the new ministry had a fair amount of success despite its short lease of life. Not only were the remaining Reform Bills and the Abyssinian expedition successful, but acts of legislation abolished church rates (in this case a Liberal bill acquiesced in by the Government), terminated public hanging, and encouraged urban slum clearance. Disraeli also built on the favourable attitude of the Queen towards him by establishing a famous friendship, which was to stand him in good stead during his much longer Government of the 1870s. What had once been Victoria's coolness or indifference towards him had been changed to warm regard by a graceful tribute he had paid in Parliament to Prince Albert after the latter's death in 1861. As premier his writing skill was used repeatedly and effectively to form and sustain an intimacy with his unlikely 'Faery'. Against his engaging epistolary ability and his honeyed tongue, Gladstone's involved and prolix verbal and written addresses did not amuse Her Majesty. At a time when royal power had dwindled almost to token status it was not, of course, essential for Disraeli to bask in the Queen's personal favour, but it must have given no little boost to his morale to do so.

So success in different respects followed Disraeli from 1867 into his premiership. But the success was not sustained for long. The question of Ireland, highlighted on the one hand by Fenian republicanism and on the other by a constitutional demand for ecclesiastical and land reforms, was again at the forefront of politics. The Conservative ministry was attempting to go some way to meet the Irish Catholic claims by offering to establish a Catholic university. This plan was initially encouraged by Henry Edward Manning, Archbishop of Westminster, but when Gladstone, in March 1868, produced the much more alluring policy of disestablishing the Church of Ireland, Manning and the Irish Catholic hierarchy gave their strong support to him. The Conservative university scheme had no hope of success in view of the increased demands now made by the hierarchy for control over the proposed institution. Disraeli took literary revenge for Manning's defection by portraying him as the devious Cardinal Grandison in his next novel, *Lothair*, written after the electoral defeat which was caused by the success of Gladstone's disestablishment challenge.

Disraeli found the Irish support which he had tried (in the wake of Russell's Ecclesiastical Titles Act) to nurture for the Conservatives, slipping back decisively to the Liberals. Some Conservatives such as Stanley and Sir John Pakington (both cabinet ministers) did not want to resist Irish disestablishment, and Disraeli himself was reluctant to take up the cudgels for the established status of the Irish Church: 'there is no doubt', he told Lord Chancellor Cairns, '[that] it is not popular'.[19] In the early debates on the question in 1868 Cranborne accused him, not altogether unjustly, of being ready to swallow Irish disestablishment just as he had accepted wide enfranchisement the previous year: he was 'an adventurer . . . without principles and honesty'.[20] Disraeli certainly had his misgivings on the issue, but he overcame them, giving a firm defence of the Irish establishment, and of establishment in general, in the many speeches he made on the question in 1868 and 1869.

Gladstone announced his intended disestablishment policy in the Commons on 16 March 1868, and tabled resolutions a week later. The resolutions were carried, and shortly afterwards there commenced a prolonged and vociferous run-up to a general election, which awaited completion of the new electoral registers. The developing contest was concerned very largely with the disestablishment issue. Sandwiched between two High Church opponents, Cranborne (Marquess of Salisbury from April 1868) and Gladstone, the premier appeared to act as a champion of extreme Evangelicalism during this contest, which he described to the very Protestant Queen as 'a great Protestant struggle'. In August he caused a stir by appointing Canon Hugh McNeile, a well-known Liverpool anti-Catholic propagandist, to the Deanery of Ripon.

When the elections finally came in November, Conservatives could face them with the nucleus of a nation-wide party organisation, the National Union of Conservative Associations, founded in late 1867.[21] The more divided Liberals did not found a similar federation until 1877, but the National Union, whose inception owed nothing to Disraeli, was as yet too undeveloped to do a great deal to aid the Conservatives' electoral performance. The Liberals went well ahead in the elections. Gladstone lost his own seat but soon found another, and he led his party to victory by 110 seats. Nonconformists, Catholics and most Whigs had supported him, and Liberal unity was temporarily established by Irish disestablishment. Disraeli resigned immediately after the contest, and Gladstone accepted the royal commission to form a Government. For Disraeli, the heady euphoria of 1867 had dissipated amid the galling set-backs of 1868. His first, brief taste of the premiership was over, and he was back in all too familiar Opposition. He declined an earldom, which he could have received as an ex-Prime Minister. But he asked for a peerage for his now aged wife, and Mary Anne became Viscountess Beaconsfield, her title displaying the Buckinghamshire connection.

.   .   .

RECESSION AND RENEWAL, 1869–74

Having met with a decisive defeat, Disraeli had to reconcile himself to what would probably be a lengthy spell of Liberal administration. For a few years, although he played his parliamentary part against government bills, he was not particularly active in confronting the situation, and illness and literary pursuits distracted him. During the sessions of 1869, 1870 and 1871 he had to be absent from the Commons on a number of occasions through ill-health. During 1869 he was writing *Lothair*, his first novel since the 1840s. Published by Longman in May 1870, this had the vast and rapid sales which were to be expected of the first novel by an ex-premier (there has only been one other, and this was by Disraeli again in 1880). Illustrating current international politics and religious controversy, the book had anti-Catholic overtones which later made it seem a lighter, fictional parallel to the vehement anti-papalism of Gladstone's *Vatican Decrees* pamphlet of 1874.

The new Conservative organisation expanded effectively from 1870, when Disraeli appointed John Gorst as party agent. As to the conduct of opposition to Gladstone, Disraeli advised (as he wrote to Stanley in January 1869) 'the utmost reserve and quietness' for the time being.[22] The Irish disestablishment bill dominated the 1869 session. Conservatives, though helpless to resist the measure in the Commons, used their majority in the Lords, amid heated relations between the two Houses, to obtain a more favourable financial settlement for the Church of Ireland than ministers had intended. There was more hope for the Opposition in 1870, when a major Education Bill for England and Wales, though passing successfully, aroused strong Nonconformist protests. These became more pronounced, over education and further questions of disestablishment, for the rest of the Government's period in office, playing a large part in disrupting the Liberal party. Trade unionists were dissatisfied by the legislation which affected their particular interests. Moreover, Irish calls for reform were by no means fully satisfied by disestablishment in 1869 and a Land Act in 1870, and the Home Government Association, which was to become the Home Rule party in 1873, began another serious fracture in Gladstone's united force of 1868–9.

A further encouragement to the Opposition was that the ministry could be accused of neglecting Britain's overseas interests. In 1871 the Opposition supported the Government over the settlement of compensation claims arising from the American Civil War, though much of public opinion condemned the arrangement as over-generous. Conservatives themselves berated ministers for their inaction during the Franco–Prussian War, when Russia took advantage of the European situation to launch its warships on the Black Sea, contravening the Treaty of Paris in 1856. This breach of an international agreement could be seen as a potential revival of Russia's threat to British interests in the eastern Mediterranean area, and it was doubtless thought that Palmerston would have acted far differently from Gladstone's passive attitude towards it.

Thus by 1871 the Government was weakening through internal division and some dissatisfaction with its foreign policy. The Conservatives were thereby encouraged to emerge from 'utmost reserve and quietness' and take a more positive and confident line of opposition. But Disraeli was not yet ready for a stronger approach, and his continued preference for quietness began to cause impatience among some of his colleagues, just as Disraeli had been impatient with Derby in the 1850s for the same reason. The Marquess of Salisbury (formerly Viscount Cranborne) remained Disraeli's chief opponent in the party, though he was not willing to pose a challenge for the leadership, probably because he seemed unlikely to get much support. Some Conservatives had wanted Salisbury to become party leader in the House of Lords when this position was vacant at the end of 1869. The proposal was pointed directly against Disraeli, for he and Salisbury were not even on speaking terms. Salisbury, however, refused to be considered for the post, and party unity escaped the severe strain which his acceptance was likely to have caused. Stanley, now fifteenth Earl of Derby, was elected to the position, but refused to accept it. Lord Cairns was next elected; he accepted, but resigned a year later. Salisbury was then again proposed, but again unsuccessfully. The Duke of Richmond was elected as a compromise candidate and filled the post until 1876, when Disraeli, having become Earl of Beaconsfield, succeeded him.

These were minor skirmishes, in which any serious threat to Disraeli was avoided. At the beginning of 1872, however, the situation became more serious for him. At the end of January and early February several leading Conservatives, but not Disraeli and Derby, met at Burghley, the Marquess of Exeter's house near Stamford in Lincolnshire. On the suggestion of Lord Cairns, the meeting agreed, though there was some dissent, that Derby would be a more effective party leader.[23] In view of Derby's repeated insistence that he did not want such a position, and a recent statement of his that he was not even entirely committed to the Conservative party, the decision was a very strange one. It can hardly have been the result of an aristocratic desire to displace a non-aristocrat. For if the concept of essential and pure aristocratic status for a Conservative leader had been so strong, there would surely have been opposition to Disraeli's succeeding Derby as premier in 1868. Nor is it at all likely that it was simply thought that the successor to the title and estate of the former Prime Minister, who had led the party for twenty-three years, should have the most prominent role in the party. Indeed, it is difficult to believe that the decision was entirely serious. It may have been intended as a warning to Disraeli that his current behaviour was not active and determined enough, in view of the increasing hopes of Conservative electoral success. If he was to remain leader, he should show more of a leader's mettle.

If the action at Burghley was intended to stir up Disraeli to greater efforts, it had the desired effect. He had no wish to lose the leadership at a time when it was beginning to look as if a Conservative majority might be gained after a wait of over a quarter of a century. It is not known whether he was informed about the Burghley decision, but it may well have leaked out to him, and in any case there was plenty of comment in the press about the unrest in his party. He was aware that a change of approach was needed, and he adopted one from that time. Lingering remains of 'the utmost reserve and quietness' were cast aside. He set out on a more determined and constructive course. Vindication of his leadership and avoidance of the need for warnings were motivating factors in the more open challenge he began to pose to the Government.

At the opening of the 1872 session he vigorously attacked government policies. During the spring and summer he made two celebrated speeches to large Conservative audiences, at the Free Trade Hall in Manchester on 3 April and at the Crystal Palace in South London on 24 June. In the Free Trade Hall he addressed Lancashire Conservatives for three hours, describing ministers in one of his most memorable phrases as 'a range of exhausted volcanoes'. He castigated the Government for lack of commitment to Britain's overseas interests and for inadequate opposition to subversive forces in the country which wanted to overthrow the established Churches, the House of Lords, and the monarchy. Gladstone he tried to portray as practically the ally of republicans.[24] It was none other than Lord Cairns, who had suggested the Burghley motion that the party might do better under Derby, who now wrote to congratulate Disraeli:

> It was a great occasion, and the speech was as great as the occasion. . . . as regards the future, it [the speech] will live and be read not only for its sparkling vigour, but also for the deep strata of constitutional thought and reasoning which pervade it.[25]

Another Conservative gathering heard a shorter speech at the Crystal Palace. There Disraeli developed the themes of patriotism and empire and the multi-class appeal of Conservatism. The working classes, he said, were keen to maintain the greatness of their country and their empire, and could look to the Conservatives with far more confidence than to the Liberals for this purpose. He had no objection to self-government in the colonies of settlement, provided that firm bonds of imperial union were maintained, such as a common tariff and a representative imperial council in London.[26] Finally, he referred briefly to social matters, emphasising the need to improve public health and working and living conditions. Conservative Governments, he pointed out, already had a notable record in bringing about such improvements (for example in the limitation of factory working hours), and he implied that a future Conservative ministry under his lead would extend these policies.[27]

In discussing social reform, Disraeli was referring to matters which had concerned him sporadically for forty years. Imperial and foreign questions had not occupied him to any marked degree, except for periods when a particular crisis or act of policy had been involved. His references at the Crystal Palace to imperial unity indicated a growing commitment to this newly developing interest on his part. He could not have foreseen how this commitment would deepen in his next ministry, when British imperial concerns would be linked with his Asian interests, combining imperial consolidation with orientalism to produce a uniquely Disraelian sense of overseas mission.[28]

In spite of Disraeli's high-flown and fragmented rhetoric in these speeches, there was not much of a distinction to be drawn, on any objective consideration, between the Conservative aspirations he expressed and the record of the Gladstone Government. This Government was not lacking in social reforming achievement, as was shown by its education, public health, coal-mining and drink licensing measures. It did not show any desire to abandon the empire or weaken imperial unity, although Gladstone was more obviously in favour of self-government (on a gradual basis) than Disraeli. The Government's passive and conciliatory foreign policy was merely prudent and economical rather than timid; and the comprehensive army reforms of Edward Cardwell, Secretary for War, greatly improved British military efficiency. Gladstone was sympathetic neither to republicanism nor to efforts to reduce the powers of the Lords, and he clearly discouraged any attempt to take disestablishment further. But Disraeli's speeches had been concerned not so much with underlying realities as with making political statements to aid his party. The effect was considerable. His two memorable orations helped to restore Conservative morale and strengthened Conservative unity behind him. After he had delivered them there was no further hint of replacing him as leader.

Although his health was repeatedly troublesome to him, Disraeli had fairly got steam up again in his political career. Mary Anne, however, became seriously unwell, and he attended her devotedly in the months before she died in December 1872. Her death plunged him into loneliness and the need for renewed financial constraint. But neither of these spectres proved fearsome for long. Loneliness he was able to assuage by the companionship, either in person or by letter, of two charming, if ageing, sisters, Lady Bradford and Lady Chesterfield. He had known them since his youthful, socially aspiring days in the 1830s, and it was through their brother, Lord Forester, that he had obtained his nomination as a candidate for Shrewsbury in 1841. After Mary Anne died Disraeli appears to have fallen in love with the younger sister, Selina Countess of Bradford, who was fifteen years his junior. Sometimes he wrote to her two or three times a day. But she was married. With the elder sister, Anne Countess of Chesterfield, who was a widow two years his senior, he merely had an intimate friendship. He proposed marriage to her, but she wisely refused. Both sisters were Conservative aristocrats, influential in the elevated party circles of which Disraeli never became wholly a part. This would have been a compelling aspect of their attraction, but amidst his heavy burdens of statesmanship in the mid- and later 1870s the chief allurement was probably their constant readiness to give him personal and political sympathy and solace. From 1873 until his death in 1881 he wrote eleven hundred letters to Selina and five hundred to Anne, giving them a wealth of political and social information such as he had given to Sarah and Mary Anne. It is no wonder that the Duke of Richmond told Lord Cairns in 1876 that Lady Bradford 'seems to know everything, down to the minutest details of everything that passes'.[29]

Materially, also, Disraeli's initially desolate state in widowerhood did not last very long. As his wife's property was in trust he lost the aid of an income of some £5,000 p.a. and the use of the opulent Grosvenor Gate mansion. He was oppressed by loneliness in the suite of rooms at Edwards's Hotel near Hanover Square, where he resided for a time during his periods in London. But his domestic state improved from February 1874 when he leased a new home at 2, Whitehall Gardens. Moreover, his benefactor of 1862, Andrew Montagu, had relieved his financial depletion by reducing the interest he was charging him from three to two per cent.[30]

Even without these generous personal and monetary aids, Disraeli could scarcely have sunk into the doldrums after Mary Anne's demise. Politics were too compelling. He had delivered his own clarion calls earlier in 1872, and by March 1873 he was scenting electoral victory. Gladstone's ministry, already much weakened by the disaffection of sections which had formerly supported it, fell into deeper trouble. After Church and land reform in Ireland, Gladstone turned to educational reform in that country, the third prong of his pacificatory initiative. He introduced an Irish University Bill to establish a new university at Dublin which would be run by an 'undenominational' governing body and would have a strictly secular curriculum, in the hope that it would be accepted by both Catholics and Protestants. But the scheme had very little chance of success after it was almost unanimously opposed by the Irish Catholic bishops. In the Commons Disraeli said the bill was 'monstrous in its general principles, pernicious in many of its details, and utterly futile as a measure of practical legislation'.[31] On 12 March a combination of Conservatives and Irish Catholics and some others overthrew the measure in the Commons by a majority of three, 287 to 284.

Like Disraeli before him, Gladstone had failed to resolve the extremely thorny Irish university question. He resigned. But Disraeli twice refused the Queen's invitation to form a ministry. He was not prepared to embark on yet a fourth minority Government which might only enable its opponents to re-unite and turn it out in an early general election. A majority big enough to keep the Conservatives in government, preferably for a full seven-year term, was what he wanted. In order to obtain more chance of achieving this, it would be better if Gladstone were compelled to resume office in circumstances unsatisfactory to his ministry. During a Gladstonian restoration, the Conservatives, who had been doing well in by-elections, might continue to thrive on the Government's problems and strengthen their prospects of success in a general election contest.

This did indeed happen. Gladstone was compelled to take up the reins of government again, and he was unable to stiffen his ranks effectively or brighten his prospects. The Conservatives, on the other hand, continued to prosper. The tide of by-elections continued to favour them. Disraeli scored a personal triumph in the unlikely ambience of radical Glasgow in November 1873, when he made a postponed visit to that city in order to be installed as Lord Rector of the university. This was an office to which he had been elected by the students two years before, probably in gratitude for the creation of Scottish university seats in his 1868 Reform Act for Scotland. He naturally disliked the persistent habit of returning a Liberal majority from Scotland, and he had unpleasant memories of youthful visits there in 1825 over the ill-fated affair of *The Representative*. But he had undertaken a more successful excursion, to address Glasgow Conservatives, in 1867, and he had first visited Balmoral in 1868. In 1873 he made several speeches in which he repeated his Manchester and Crystal Palace triumphs and more recent oratorical attacks he had been making on the Government. Praising the successful commercial spirit of Glasgow and the patriotic spirit of Scotland, he concluded an address to the city's Conservative Association by calling on it to help 'to guard civilization alike from the withering blast of atheism and from the simoom of sacerdotal usurpation':

> If that struggle comes, we must look to Scotland to aid us. It was once, and I hope is still, a land of liberty, of patriotism, and of religion. I think the time has come when it really should leave off mumbling the dry bones of political economy and munching the remainder biscuit of an effete Liberalism. We all know that a General Election is at hand. . . . I ask you, when the occasion comes, to act as becomes an ancient and famous nation, and give all your energies for the cause of faith and freedom.[32]

Although his terms were characteristically high-flown and romanticised, Disraeli pleased many in his audiences and he was re-elected as Lord Rector for a second term in 1874.

By January 1874 Gladstone had hit on one of his favourite notions, that of abolishing the income tax, as a means of trying to re-unite the Liberals and steer them to electoral victory. With this cry he announced the dissolution of Parliament and an appeal to the country. His effort fell flat. Most of the electorate were not liable to income tax, and even tax-payers would be wary of supporting a policy which was rather too obviously pulled out of the hat for electoral purposes. The fractiousness in his party clearly remained, and indeed intensified, during the general election in February. The tax proposal indeed created a new reason for Liberal division by alarming radicals who wanted more government spending on social improvement.

In the election the Conservatives benefited more from Liberal disharmony than from any positive policies of their own. Disraeli's lofty expressions in his speeches of 1872 had not been translated into any definite, detailed intentions. His election manifesto was fairly unconstructive. It concentrated on attacking Gladstone's 'incessant and harassing legislation' and his alleged radical extremism, though it did emphasise the importance of a patriotic defence of Britain's world-wide interests. The Conservatives had the benefit of a stronger electoral organisation than their opponents, thanks to the activity of the Conservative Central Office and the National Union of Conservative Associations. The results gave the Conservatives 350 seats, the Liberals 245, and the new Irish Home Rule party fifty-seven. It was an overall majority of forty-eight – not a tremendous leap, but significant as the first time the Conservatives had had a majority since 1846 and probably sufficient to keep them in power for some years. Disraeli would no doubt have said that he had climbed to the top of the greasy pole, if he had not already said it in 1868.

Gladstone resigned and Disraeli accepted the Queen's commission for the second time on 18 February. To Disraeli, it was the well-earned reward of constant striving, self-assertion and seizure of opportunities. His unremitting efforts had first given him the leadership of his party in the Commons, then the premiership, and finally the premiership with a majority.

.   .   .

NOTES

1. R. Blake, *Disraeli*, London 1966, p. 437.
2. Ibid., pp. 437–44.
3. W.F. Monypenny and G.E. Buckle, vol. IV, p. 440 *The Life of Benjamin Disraeli, Earl of Beaconsfield*, 6 vols, London 1910–20 (hereafter cited as Monypenny & Buckle).

4. M. Cowling, 'Disraeli, Derby and fusion, October 1865 to July 1866', *Historical Journal*, vol. VIII, 1965, pp. 31–71.
5. R.W. Davis, *Disraeli*, London 1976, p. 148.
6. Blake, *Disraeli*, pp. 451–3.
7. Davis, *Disraeli*, p. 149.
8. Blake, *Disraeli*, pp. 456–60.
9. Ibid., p. 463; F.B. Smith, *The Making of the Second Reform Bill*, Cambridge 1966, pp. 161–4.
10. Blake, *Disraeli*, p. 473.
11. P. Smith, *Disraelian Conservatism and Social Reform*, London 1967, p. 86; for a detailed treatment of the Government's social measures in 1867, see also pp. 46–72.
12. Ibid., p. 65.
13. Monypenny & Buckle, vol. V, pp. 43–4. See Freda Harcourt, 'Disraeli's imperialism, 1866–8: a question of timing', *Historical Journal*, vol. XXIII, 1980, pp. 87–109.
14. Monypenny & Buckle, vol. IV, p. 585.
15. See the correspondence ibid., pp. 585–90.
16. Ibid., pp. 588–9.
17. R. Shannon, *The Age of Disraeli, 1868–81: the rise of Tory democracy*, London 1992, pp. 29–31. See the different view in Blake, *Disraeli*, p. 486.
18. For example, J. Vincent (ed.) *Disraeli, Derby and the Conservative Party: journals and memoirs of Edward Henry, Lord Stanley, 1849–69*, Hassocks 1978, pp. 248, 328–9.
19. Quoted in G.I.T. Machin, *Politics and the Churches in Great Britain, 1832 to 1868*, Oxford 1977, p. 361.
20. Quoted in Blake, *Disraeli*, p. 499.
21. For the new Conservative organisation and its development, see E.J. Feuchtwanger, *Disraeli, Democracy and the Tory Party: Conservative leadership and organisation after the Second Reform Bill*, Oxford 1968, p. 105ff.; Shannon, *The Age of Disraeli*, p. 15ff.
22. Quoted in Monypenny & Buckle, vol. V, p. 103. See also Vincent, *Disraeli, Derby and the Conservative Party*, pp. 339, 347.
23. Shannon, *The Age of Disraeli*, pp. 111–13.
24. Monypenny & Buckle, vol. V, pp. 186–92; Smith, *Disraelian Conservatism and Social Reform*, pp. 155–61.
25. Cairns to Disraeli, 6 April 1872; Disraeli Papers, Bodleian Library, 91/2, fos 15–16.
26. C.C. Eldridge, *England's Mission: the imperial idea in the*

age of Gladstone and Disraeli, 1868–80, London 1973, pp. 172–86.

27. Monypenny & Buckle, vol. V, pp. 193–6.
28. Eldridge, *England's Mission*, pp. 173–7, 209.
29. Monypenny & Buckle, vol. V, p. 241; Sarah Bradford, *Disraeli*, London 1982, p. 307ff.
30. Monypenny & Buckle, vol. V, pp. 232–3.
31. Quoted in G.I.T. Machin, *Politics and the Churches in Great Britain, 1869 to 1921*, Oxford 1987, p. 54.
32. B. Disraeli, *Inaugural Address delivered to the University of Glasgow, November 19, 1873* (second edition, including the occasional speeches at Glasgow), London 1873, pp. 68–9.

Chapter 6

STRUGGLE WITH GLADSTONE, 1874–1881

. . .

APOGEE, 1874–8

Disraeli began his Indian summer when he was nearly seventy. He had reached vintage maturity, but was increasingly plagued by illnesses – gout, bronchitis and asthma – which caused him to pass sleepless nights. If he sometimes nodded off at cabinet meetings this may not have been, as has sometimes been alleged, because he was bored with the proceedings (especially when the prosaic details of social reform measures were being discussed), but simply because he was weak or tired. By 1876 his parliamentary performance was clearly deteriorating, making him vulnerable to criticism, but he seems to have had no difficulty in maintaining a general domination over his Cabinet. He was constantly occupied, as far as his physical state allowed. Frequent dinner parties and a full correspondence took up much of his leisure time. He said after his election victory that power had come to him too late, but this is highly doubtful. Mentally he was as alert as ever, and he conducted his administration with vigour, imagination and success. Even in the final two years of governmental decline the failures were substantially brought on him by others. Until these difficulties arose after 1878 he sprung surprises, scored triumphs, and passed much useful legislation.

Disraeli formed a strong, talented ministry. He re-united leading Conservatives after their division in 1867 by obtaining the services of the Marquess of Salisbury (as Secretary for India) and the Earl of Carnarvon (as Colonial Secretary). If these two symbolised Conservative reunion, the inclusion of Richard Assheton Cross, a Lancashire solicitor and business man, as Home Secretary symbolised the increasing and valuable accession of prosperous middle-class support to the Conservative party. Salisbury agreed to re-join Disraeli only with reluctance: 'the prospect of having to serve with this man again is like a nightmare', he told his wife.[1] However, even his sensitive High Churchmanship was somewhat re-assured in conversation with Disraeli, though in the coming parliamentary session a divisive ecclesiastical bill strained their alliance again. After this episode their relations im-proved, and Salisbury eventually gave Disraeli a great deal of help in foreign policy. Carnarvon, however, who had left the Government with Salisbury in 1867 and joined the new one with him in 1874, disagreed strongly with Disraeli's foreign policy and resigned in 1878. Ironically Derby, the premier's close friend of long standing and Foreign Secretary, also became alienated from him over the same issues. He resigned soon after Carnarvon and was succeeded by Salisbury at the Foreign Office.

Thus the history of the Cabinet became quite a turbulent one. But Disraeli could almost invariably count on the support of the Queen. Through his attractive writing of reports and his blatant verbal flattery he built on the firm friendship they had been forming during his last Government. They established a relationship of strong mu-tual sympathy in both a personal and a political sense. There were occasions, however, when the friendship encouraged Victoria to be highly ambitious, even dictatorial, and Disraeli was not always able to control the relationship exactly as he wished.

In spite of the purposeful tone of Disraeli's two famous speeches of 1872, the new premier had no programme of action. Richard Cross was disconcerted to find that one who had delivered these speeches had no legislative plans whatever, and was entirely reliant on the suggestions of his colleagues.[2] This would have been no surprise, however, to those who knew Disraeli's lack of interest in planning and his reliance on improvisation. Power had come to the Conservative party through the divisions of its opponents rather than through any declared policies of its own. During its first parliamentary session, beginning on 19 March 1874, the Government was led into ecclesiastical turbulence and fractiousness by two bills, both of which had government sponsorship and both of which were unsuccessful in their objects. These were respectively intended to defend the Church of Scotland and the Church of England.

In Scotland, Conservatives hoped to weaken the reigning Liberalism by strengthening the established Church, whose ministers, as had been shown in the recent election, generally voted in their favour. Successive secessions since the 1730s had placed over half the Scottish Presbyterians outside the establishment, mainly in the Free Church and the United Presbyterian Church. Protests against lay patronage in the appointment of ministers in the Church of Scotland had ostensibly caused the Disruption and the formation of the Free Church in 1843, and it was hoped that the abolition of patronage in the establishment would win back Free Churchmen to its fold. The Patronage Bill which was introduced in the Lords on 18 May, and for which Disraeli spoke when it was in the Commons, was intended to achieve this. But instead of doing so it aroused the ire of Free Churchmen who did not believe there was sufficient spiritual independence in the Church of Scotland to persuade them to return to it. Gladstone supported them in this opposition and delivered a strong attack on the bill in the Commons on 6 July, although his attitude helped to maintain religious divisions among the Liberals. The bill was enacted on 7 August, but already an intense dispute over disestablishment was growing in Scotland. This continued for over a decade, during which time it formed the main political question there. The Patronage Act did not strengthen the Scottish Church establishment as intended, but made it more vulnerable to attack.[3]

Gladstone attended the Commons little in the 1874 session. But he visited the House again on 9 July, three days after he had attacked the Scottish Patronage Bill, in order to denounce the Public Worship Regulation Bill which was directed against certain ritualistic practices in the Church of England. Gladstone, though a Tractarian or Anglo-Catholic, did not see the need for extravagance of ritual, but said he defended the ritualists because he disliked intolerant treatment of them. The question of what action to take, if any, against the growth of unauthorised ritualist practices, had become a major point of controversy before Disraeli's ministry was formed. The new premier had assured

Salisbury that there would not be a government bill against ritualism. Nevertheless when an anti-ritualist bill was introduced in the Lords on 20 April by Archibald Tait, Archbishop of Canterbury, strongly supported by the Queen, Disraeli, after initial reluctance, gave it his full backing. After passing through the Lords the bill entered the Commons in early July. Gladstone denounced it vigorously on the ninth, but the measure passed. Its impression of stark secular coercion of clergy by the State was sufficiently modified by its actual provisions to keep a grumbling Salisbury, Carnarvon and other High Churchmen in the Government. But the Act caused controversy for many years and its attempt to enforce a strict observance of the Prayer Book was unsuccessful. Recalcitrant clergy who refused to abandon illegal ritual were imprisoned over the next eight years. But coercion failed and their movement spread, producing an unsuccessful attempt to pass another law against them in the early twentieth century.[4]

Disraeli's Government got off to a bad start through these ecclesiastical bills. The embarrassment they caused lasted throughout the ministry and beyond, as it was revealed how far both were from realising their aims. The particular attitudes of High Churchmen in the Government, highlighted by the Public Worship Regulation Bill, were linked to their reactions in the Russo–Turkish crisis a few years later, in which their religious sympathies were with the Orthodox Church.

. . .

The new ministry had more fruitful success during its first session in making a beginning with social reform. Concentration on this branch of legislation continued in the sessions of 1875 and 1876, forming the Government's most constructive domestic contribution. From the middle of 1876 ministers had to turn their concentration, with eventual if partial success, onto another major theme of Disraeli's speeches of 1872, that of imperial and foreign defence.

As already suggested, the author of *Sybil* and the one-time opponent of the Poor Law had a genuine and lasting interest in social improvement; though with him it was, as in the case of the empire, sporadic rather than continuous, and a matter of broad conception and vision rather than one of dedicated attention to detail. The latter was not usually his *forte*, though he had paid much attention to detailed planning in the case of Parliamentary Reform. In matters of social improvement he recognised the essential importance of detail but was glad to leave it to those who were more expert at it.

Despite the lack of legislative plans for social reform when he took office, the new premier would have been the first to agree that the Conservatives had to adopt constructive reform measures if they were to gain and retain power in an increasingly populist age. But he was not the man to draft and issue blueprints. His strength lay in broad ideas, sharp perceptions, and swift and startling interventions. He often looked to others to complement these attributes with the more mundane and deliberate virtues of planning, drafting, and even suggesting in the first place what measures to introduce. He had no conception of a coherent, progressive programme of reforms, and the social bills of his Governments were introduced empirically to deal with individual problems. It was a hand-to-mouth effort, far removed from anything like planning a Welfare State. The actual measures fell particularly to Richard Cross at the Home Office. Other important social contributions came from George Sclater-Booth at the Local Government Board, Viscount Sandon at the Education Department, and Sir Charles Adderley at the Board of Trade.[5]

Cross's initiative was behind all the three government social moves in the 1874 session – a Royal Commission to consider trade union legislation, over which Gladstone's Government had dissatisfied the unions; an Act confirming a working day of no more than ten hours for all factory workers; and a controversial Intoxicating Liquors Act, which modified the Licensing Act of 1872 in the interests of the brewers and publicans, who had reputedly flocked to vote for Conservative candidates in the recent election.

Most of the ministry's social reforms were introduced and enacted in the following session of 1875. Like the factory and licensing legislation of 1874, these were not restricted by a permissive approach but showed considerable willingness to develop State compulsion. Nevertheless there was a decided element of *laissez-faire* about most of the reforms, perhaps reflecting the fact that the Conservatives were looking for increasing middle-class support. The combination of compulsory and permissive elements reflected the mixed approaches which characterised nineteenth-century social legislation – direct, centralised State enforcement running parallel to devolved concessions to traditional decision-making by local bodies. The more compulsory of the 1875 measures included Sclater-Booth's Public Health Act, which gathered many earlier provisions into one statute, and another Factory Act to place additional curbs on the exploitation of women and children. Sclater-Booth's Sale of Food and Drugs Act, to establish standards of nutritional and medicinal content and to prevent adulteration, was inadequate in its compulsory powers until these were extended in 1879; and Florence Nightingale may have been initially over-optimistic in writing: 'Under the new "Adulteration Laws" poor Baby will have a better chance of getting beyond babyhood than now, we hope'.[6]

Also of compulsory application were the labour laws of 1875. These have been described by the authority on Disraelian social legislation as 'easily the most important of the government's social reforms'; and Disraeli, jubilant at their passage, expected them to 'gain and retain for the Tories the lasting affection of the working classes'.[7] The new laws, both of them bipartisan measures extended by successful Liberal amendments, were Cross's Conspiracy and Protection of Property Act, which legalised peaceful picketing, and the same minister's Employers and Workmen Act which (with some exceptions) freed workers from liability to criminal prosecution for breach of contract.[8]

Cross's Artisans Dwelling Act, on the other hand, sought to encourage housing improvements but emphasised local decision by merely enabling, and not compelling, municipal authorities to carry these out. The effects of permissiveness, together with the high cost of making these improvements, were shown when, six years later, only ten of the eighty-seven towns in England and Wales to which the Act applied had made any attempt to put its provisions into operation.[9] Also not very strong or efficacious was a Friendly Societies Act, prepared by Cross and Sir Stafford

Northcote (Chancellor of the Exchequer), which made a rather minimal effort to ensure greater financial reliability among these bodies.

Several more social measures were passed in 1876. Sclater-Booth's very limited Rivers Pollution Act took the first hesitating steps by a Government towards encouraging riverine cleanliness. Similarly, Sir Charles Adderley's Merchant Shipping Act, passed after a struggle of some years and the abandonment of a much-disputed bill in 1875, went only a limited way in the direction of satisfying the determined campaigner Samuel Plimsoll and his followers from different political parties. Lord Sandon's Education Act, on the other hand, gave compulsory powers to local authorities for the enforcement of elementary school attendance. This Act was mainly intended to aid the Anglican and Roman Catholic voluntary schools against the encroachment of board schools championed by Nonconformists. In connection with the controversy over it, Disraeli gave another example of the unpredictable variability of his attitude to ecclesiastical matters when he wrote to the Queen:

> the Ministry fell into one of those messes of ecclesiastical weakness, which seems inevitable, every now and then, for the Conservative party. The whole of yesterday was consequently wasted on an idle Education clause, which conveyed a petty assault on the Nonconformists.[10]

After these measures of 1876 the Government's social reforming urge, impressive while it lasted, had almost spent itself. Except for Cross's consolidatory Factory Act of 1878 there was very little in the ministry's later years to compare with the numerous social reforming successes of 1874–6. A number of social issues was tackled in the later sessions, but an Act very rarely resulted, and if it did it was of only minor consequence. In social reform matters as in other fields, anti-climax afflicted the Government by the end of the 1870s.

The large cluster of social Acts did not produce any collective revolutionary change, and was not intended to do so. It was meant to deal with a range of particular problems, not least in the hope of gaining political support from different sections of society. But it did form a constructive and distinctive achievement by the Government, paralleled only by the attainments of its overseas policy. It was marked by convention in that permissiveness was often applied, but there were also some bold strokes advancing State compulsion.

It is spurious, however, to attempt to elevate and dignify these reforms by the attribution of a philosophic approach called 'Tory democracy', which is meant also to include the Reform Act and the social reforms of 1867–8. The Reform Act of 1867 and its associated electoral measures appeared very restricted when measured alongside democratic values. The social reforms of 1867–8 and of the mid-1870s, moreover, were not really democratic at all in the proper sense of the term, for they were not concerned with giving political power to the people, but with improving their living, working, and environmental conditions. They could have been introduced without being accompanied by any extension of electoral participation. There was not Liberal democracy at this time, and nor was there Tory.

If 'Tory democracy' is meant to imply bestowal by the aristocracy of benefits on the people in order to win their support for the maintenance of aristocratic power, it is also unconvincing as a description of Conservative policy at this time. The Conservative party was now becoming rather less aristocratic and more middle-class in its leadership and control, and was increasingly subject to the same tensions and conflicts which the Liberal party experienced between employers and workers. Both the Liberals and Conservatives were looking for support from both the middle and the working classes, and both parties had to contend with economic and social divisions among their supporters.

Nor can the group of social Acts, any more than the Reform Act and associated measures, be seen as embodying a development which was unique to Disraeli and his ministries. They extended a well-established nineteenth-century practice whereby both Liberal and Conservative Governments passed such measures, with the object of removing grievances, obviating political protest, and gaining electoral support. By the 1870s the recent enfranchisement of skilled workers had emphasised the political importance of this section of society and its needs. The social legislation of Disraeli's ministry, however, proved disappointing as a means (which Disraeli hoped it would be) of winning substantial support from this section for the Conservatives.

. . .

The session of 1876, like that of 1875, was a great success for Disraeli. But throughout this highly satisfying period the Prime Minister was repeatedly troubled by illness, and his critics did not forbear to question the effectiveness of his leadership. 'In the ordinary conduct of business Disraeli shows himself at every turn quite incompetent to guide the House', wrote Sir William Heathcote, a former Conservative MP, in April 1876 to Salisbury (who, in spite of his reconciliation with Disraeli, would probably not have been sorry to hear such comments).[11] Disraeli was indeed conscious of his increasing ineffectiveness in the Commons, caused by illness, and he considered either resigning the premiership or going to the Lords. He might have resigned if Derby had agreed to succeed him, but Derby predictably declined to perform the role. Disraeli therefore continued in office but decided to take a peerage and conduct his premiership from the quieter ambience of the Upper House. He obtained the approval of his cabinet colleagues for this action. On 11 August 1876 he made a final, very important speech in his beloved Commons, the scene of so many of his triumphs, on the intensely controversial *cause célèbre* of the Bulgarian atrocities and on his determination to uphold the British Empire. Next day it was officially announced that the Queen had created him Earl of Beaconsfield. At the beginning of the following session he took his seat in the Lords.

By taking a peerage Disraeli set a seal on his attainment of power and eminence. He also declined somewhat in everyday prominence. The House of Commons had long been the main theatre of British political activity, and the continuous rivalry of Disraeli and Gladstone within its walls had emphasised its primacy. After Disraeli's mastery of the Commons, Beaconsfield's actions in the Lords could only seem like semi-retirement. He realised that he would probably remain premier for a few more years, but, per-suaded by uncertain health, he had chosen thenceforth to discharge his parliamentary duties in the more restful purlieus of the peers.

Although the premier was seeking to make his life less demanding, the next two years were among the most turbulent of his career, being rivalled in this respect only by 1845–6 and 1867. Overseas affairs, and especially Britain's imperial interests, had come to dominate his political scene. Disraeli found much more opportunity than he had probably bargained for in 1872 to vindicate the imperial sentiments he had then delivered. At the same time as his Government was fulfilling the social sentiments of those speeches, it became desirable to fulfil the imperial intentions as well.

For most of his career Disraeli had perforce acted as a critic of the foreign policies of others rather than initiating ones of his own. In the era of Palmerstonian assertiveness he had voted alongside Cobdenite pacifists even if he was conscious that he had more in common with Palmerston than with them. In the early 1870s he had taken the opposite approach of attacking Gladstone for his alleged indifference to Britain's position in the world. It was as if he was now attempting to fill the void left by Palmerston in the conduct of overseas affairs, at the same time reviving the feud which had existed between Palmerston and Gladstone.

Startling and successful overseas *coups* had been characteristic of Palmerston, and they became characteristic of Disraeli during his periods in government in 1867–8 and in the 1870s. During his ministry of the 1870s his commitment to upholding the might and influence of Britain was all the firmer because this aim was strongly linked to defending Turkey and India. These areas aroused the strong oriental enthusiasms of one who had travelled in the eastern Mediterranean region, the cradle of his race, and had filled some of his novels with eastern romance. His imperial interests developed all the more because of the oriental emphasis they were given in the 1870s. He had never shown much interest in the settled, self-governing colonies, though he wanted to keep them attached to the Empire. Nor was he much concerned with the detailed problems of imperial government. He was interested in imperialism because of the impression it could make on the world in raising British prestige, and because of the enthusiasm which would be aroused at home for a Government which pursued it successfully.[12] Like Palmerston, he was no pursuer of long-term, gruelling expansion, but rather a seeker for instant glory through the performance of spectacular *coups* which would confirm and enhance Britain's pre-eminence in the world.

The defence of Britain's Indian empire, and of her interests in the Levant (or eastern Mediterranean area) which included the new and rapidly developing British approach to India, were at the heart of most of Disraeli's overseas concerns in the 1870s. The Suez Canal, opened in 1869, was becoming the preferred sea-route to India because it offered a much shorter journey than the traditional route round the Cape of Good Hope. By 1875 four-fifths of the canal's traffic was British, and Disraeli's most dazzling *coup* was the British Government's purchase of forty-four per cent of the shares in the canal in November that year. He had shown an active interest in such a purchase since the start of his Government. In 1875 the bankruptcy of the Sultan of Turkey hastened that of his nominal vassal the Khedive of Egypt, who was almost as free-spending as his nominal overlord. The Khedive owned forty-four per cent of the Suez Canal shares, and he began to negotiate with French syndicates for the sale of these in order to stave off financial ruin. The remainder of the canal shares (forming a clear majority) was already in French hands, and it would not be at all in British interests if the canal became wholly French-owned, as imperial rivalry between the two countries might some day prevent Britain using it.

Disraeli heard that the Khedive's shares were for sale. It was his decision that 'the thing must be done', as he told the Queen – meaning that the British Government must purchase the shares. He carried the Cabinet with him. The French competition to buy the shares fell through. On 23 November the Khedive agreed to sell the shares to the British Government for four million pounds. Baron Rothschild advanced this amount to the Government at what seemed an exorbitant rate of interest. On 24 November the Prime Minister was able to tell the Queen: 'It is just settled; you have it, Madam'.[13]

There were all the ingredients of Disraelian romance, imagination and fulfilment in this affair – oriental political advantage within grasp; swift personal decisions; secret and successful negotiations; a familiar need to ignore high interest rates; and a triumphant conclusion he could loyally report to his 'Faery'. It was altogether high-class cloak and dagger. With typical hyperbole he exulted to Lady Bradford: 'We have had all the gamblers, capitalists, financiers of the world organized and platooned in bands of plunderers, arrayed against us, and secret emissaries in every corner, and have baffled them all'.[14]

The share purchase symbolised the strong British commitment to India, and to maintaining the Ottoman empire as both a protection and a gateway to India. This commitment motivated Disraeli's Government amidst the international concern with Turkey and its rebellious provinces from 1875. 'It is now *the Canal and India*; there is no such thing now to us as India alone. India is any number of cyphers; but the Canal is the unit that makes these cyphers valuable.' Thus wrote Cairns to Disraeli in January 1876.[15] The imperial significance of India was emphasised by the Prince of Wales's visit there in the winter of 1875–6, and by the passing of an Act in 1876 giving the Queen – at her strong behest, and against strong parliamentary opposition – the title of Empress of India.[16]

In July 1875 troubles had commenced in the Turkish empire which began to pose a threat of foreign intervention and, in consequence, a threat to Britain's position in the eastern Mediterranean and India. The threat came, as it had done previously, from Russia. Panslavist ideas were already encouraging Russian intervention in Turkey's Balkan provinces. In the general circumstances of Russian imperial ambition and advance in that period, it was not too far-fetched to believe that, if Russia captured Constantinople, she might go on to annex other parts of Turkey, develop sea power in the eastern Mediterranean and threaten the Suez Canal. As a Central Asian parallel to Russian threats to encroach on the Ottoman empire, Russian military successes since 1868 against the khanates of Turkestan (the area of Bokhara, Samarkand and Tashkent) had led to her annexation of territory or the creation of vassal states in that region. This brought the virtual Russian frontier south to Afghanistan and northern India. If Russia harboured a long-term ambition to confront and outstrip Britain in the search for imperial glory, an advance by her into the

Balkans and towards Constantinople, another advance into Turkish Armenia from the Caucasus, and further advances in Central Asia to the north of Afghanistan and Persia, might be the dangerous beginnings of such a confrontation on several fronts. The Russian threat had not been ignored by Britain in the past. Nor was it at this juncture. Britain, under Disraeli's lead, became an important participant in the Balkan and Armenian upheavals of 1875–8 and their resolution at the Congress of Berlin.[17]

In this conflict, primarily one between Russia and Turkey, Disraeli was naturally a defender of Turkey. He had been warmly attracted to the Turks on his Mediterranean tour in 1830–1, though by the 1870s his youthful admiration had been tempered by diplomatic reality and he occasionally showed exasperation with the difficulties that Turkey caused for herself and her allies. 'All the Turks may be in the Propontis so far as I am concerned', he told Lord Derby on 6 September 1876. He was not so much pro-Turkish as a defender of British imperial interests, of which Turkey was a natural support. Gladstone took an opposite, extremely anti-Turkish position; but he was not so much pro-Russian as desirous of the establishment of independent Balkan states. Even on this basis, however, he found it impossible to bring about a notable change in British foreign policy. The battle between him and Disraeli was even fiercer than it had been in 1867, and again Disraeli emerged as the victor.

A minor revolt against Turkish government began in Herzegovina in July 1875 and had slow but widespread effects. It spread to Bosnia and gained the support of Serbia and Montenegro. Russia, Germany and Austria-Hungary began a process of urging the Sultan to reform his regime – a process which elicited many promises of reformation but virtually no action. Disraeli was reluctant to join in these international warnings. In May 1876 he and his Cabinet refused to adhere to the Berlin Memorandum which was issued to Turkey. Britain's Mediterranean fleet was sent to Besika Bay near the southern entrance to the Dardanelles (where Palmerston had twice sent it previously) in order to emphasise support for Turkey.[18] But Turkey's increasingly despotic methods of dealing with her restless and troublesome Christian subjects were a serious embarrassment to Disraeli's supportive attitude towards her. They also encouraged Gladstone to pose a vigorous and profound, but ultimately unsuccessful, challenge to Disraeli's Government.

On 23 June 1876 the news broke on the British public, conveyed by the Liberal *Daily News*, of horrifying atrocities perpetrated a month before by Turkish troops on Bulgarian peasants who had risen in revolt in the Philippopolis (Plovdiv) region and killed some officials. It was alleged that 25,000 people had been massacred in the fierce suppression. Disraeli's natural desire to defend Turkey, his equally natural dislike of the *Daily News* (which had always been hostile to him), and excessively moderate reports of the atrocities sent by the pro-Turkish ambassador in Constantinople, Sir Henry Elliot, combined to cause the Prime Minister to question the veracity of the early accounts. He did so with some justification, for the early reports proved to be exaggerated. The number of slaughtered victims was probably only half the alleged 25,000. But the murder of 12,000 people in conditions of fiendish cruelty was quite enough to merit the strong dissatisfaction shown with some of Disraeli's comments, including his famous reference to 'coffee-house babble' in the Commons on 31 July. He tried to minimise the reports of torture by referring to his first-hand knowledge, gained during his visit to Albania in 1830, about the apparent Turkish preference for summary execution in dealing with revolts. 'Daily decapitating half the province' had been one of his hyperbolic phrases in describing the Grand Vízier whom he had met in Albania at that time, when he had also expressed his strong personal admiration of the Turks.

Strong moral reaction against the Bulgarian atrocities was shown by various vocal and influential sections of public opinion, and not least by many Conservatives. Cairns wrote to Disraeli (now Beaconsfield) on 31 August: 'we should recognize and place on record our disgust at what now too truly appear to have been the almost incredible barbarities practised in Bulgaria'.[19] Gladstone eventually decided – partly in order to reunite his party, and not least to draw alienated Nonconformists back to his side – to take a leading part in the denunciations of Turkey. His intervention strengthened and prolonged the agitation and made it a serious threat to Beaconsfield's policy of defending the Ottoman empire.

On 6 September 1876 Gladstone published his most famous work, *The Bulgarian Horrors and the Question of the East*. This pamphlet sold 200,000 copies by the end of the month, and its influence was not to be brushed aside by Beaconsfield's description of it as 'of all the Bulgarian horrors perhaps the greatest'.[20] A hitherto unremarked aspect of Gladstone's pamphlet is that it was apparently lampooning, as well as denouncing, Beaconsfield's pro-Turkish proclivities. Quite recently Gladstone had read *Tancred* for the first time. There he had found passages such as the following:

> The Christians in the Druse districts were vassals of the Druse lords. The direct rule of a Christian Caimacam was an infringement on all the feudal rights of the Djinblats and Yazbecks, of the Talhooks and the Abdel-Maleks. It would be equally fatal to the feudal rights of the Christian chiefs, the Kazins and the Eldadahs, the Elheires and the El Dahers, as regarded their Druse tenantry, unless the impossible plan of the patriarch of the Maronites, which already produced a civil war, had been adopted.[21]

Gladstone was almost parodying this style when he included in his pamphlet probably the most celebrated passage he ever wrote:

> Let the Turks now carry away their abuses in the only possible manner, namely by carrying off themselves. Their Zaptiehs and their Mudirs, their Bimbashis and their Yuzbashis, their Kaimakams and their Pashas, one and all, bag and baggage, shall I hope clear out from the province they have desolated and profaned.[22]

Having a wide range of public opinion behind him, Gladstone had the best of the argument for a while. In policy terms, he wished to replace Turkish rule in the Balkans not by Russian sway but by independent national states. The lengthy conflict between the rival political leaders reached its peak of intensity in the autumn and winter of 1876–7, and stayed there for the rest of Beaconsfield's life. The latter gave vent to some fierce expressions against his opponent, for example telling Lady Bradford:

what you say about Gladstone is most just. What restlessness! What vanity! And what unhappiness must be
his! Easy to say he is mad. It looks like it. My theory
about him is unchanged: a ceaseless Tartuffe from the
beginning.[23]

Beaconsfield continued to find only the weakest defences
for the Turks, claiming for example that they were targeted
by 'the secret societies of Europe', which was his ludicrously
inadequate description of Balkan nationalism. All the force
of Gladstone's anti-Turkish rhetoric was of course lost on
the premier, who did not relax his determination that the
integrity of Turkey must, if and when it was thought
necessary, be defended against Russian encroachment.

The prospect of Russo–Turkish war began to loom menac-
ingly in November 1876. After the Turks had defeated
Serbia in a war which ended, under Russian pressure,
in an armistice at the end of October, Russian forces
began to mobilise for a possible advance into the Balkans.
Beaconsfield said in a speech at the Guildhall on 9 November, in what must surely have been taken as a model for the
famous jingo song, that Britain was determined to maintain
peace, but that 'there is no country so well prepared for war
as our own ... if the contest is one which concerns her
liberty, her independence, or her empire, her resources, I
feel, are inexhaustible'.[24] An international conference held at
Constantinople for several weeks, starting on 14 December,
failed to solve the growing crisis and ended on 20 January
1877. Russia strengthened herself in preparation for an
invasion of Turkey's Balkan provinces by forming a pact
with Austria–Hungary whereby the latter would establish
her rule over Bosnia and Herzegovina, removing these from
Turkish government.

Russia declared war on Turkey on 24 April 1877, and
commenced her invasion by sending troops across the River
Pruth into semi-independent Rumania. By this time Gladstone's agitation was weakening. His uncompromising opposition to ministerial foreign policy was unpalatable to some
of his Liberal colleagues, who feared the more threatening
position now taken by Russia, and he was significantly
defeated in the Commons on 7 May. On the other hand,
Beaconsfield did not obtain complete ministerial support

when he wished to end British neutrality and to demonstrate armed resistance to any Russian intention to capture Constantinople. This would be done by sending a fleet to anchor near Constantinople, backed up by the occupation of the Gallipoli peninsula. Derby, Salisbury and Carnarvon opposed this line of policy. Salisbury and Carnarvon, as High Churchmen, might have been moved partly by religious sympathy with the Orthodox Christian subjects of Turkey. Whereas Salisbury came round to accept Beaconsfield's policy, Carnarvon and Derby eventually left office because they remained strongly attached to neutrality. Cabinet meetings at this time were stormy, and Beaconsfield described Derby and Carnarvon as 'the Russian party' among his colleagues. Some time before he resigned in January 1878, Carnarvon delivered a public speech on the question which Beaconsfield said could have been made by Gladstone. Derby finally left the ministry in March, and became a Liberal two years later (though he split from Gladstone over Irish Home Rule in 1886).

Ironically, therefore, Beaconsfield kept the allegiance of Salisbury, his main Conservative foe in 1867, and lost that of Derby, his intimate friend and one-time political acolyte. Derby's opinion was that Russia was engaging in war only in order to obtain better treatment for Turkey's Christian subjects. Bellicose moves by Britain might only provoke her to destroy the Turkish empire, and Britain emphatically did not want this result. Beaconsfield, however, believed that a firm stand by Britain, backed up by a demonstration of military might, was essential in order to deter the Tsar from trying to capture Constantinople. This view was held much more strongly by the Queen, who impressed it on him in numerous letters.

In the early stages of the war 'the Tsar's liberating armies' made steady progress. But after crossing the Danube their advance was held up for several months from the end of July 1877 by strong Turkish resistance led by Osman Pasha at Plevna in northern Bulgaria; though in contrast to this setback the Russians captured towns such as Batum and Kars in their parallel campaign in Armenia. It seemed that the Russians, frustrated in their first Balkan campaign, might launch a second after the winter. Beaconsfield, in a move known to the Queen but not to the Cabinet, informed the Tsar, Alexander II, that the Cabinet was united in support of British military intervention if such a campaign was commenced. In fact, however, the Cabinet was not entirely in favour of such a policy, so the Prime Minister's action was not fully warranted. His problems over ministerial divisions and war policy were compounded by physical indispositions which assailed him in the autumn – Bright's disease, bronchitis, asthma, insomnia, and indigestion. He did, however, now have much more support for a policy of warlike readiness from a public which was considerably impressed by the Turkish successes at Plevna – even if this opinion sometimes appeared in the 'jingo' terms of the music-hall ditty which can hardly have been to his taste.

On 9 December the Russian forces finally overcame the Plevna resistance and resumed their southward progress, capturing Sofia and steadily advancing closer to the Ottoman capital. The advance continued until an armistice was signed at Adrianople on 31 January 1878. Before this, Beaconsfield had carried three resolutions in Cabinet proposing British intervention, causing both Carnarvon and Derby to resign, though Derby agreed after an uncertain few days to with-draw his resignation and remained in the Government until March.

On the basis of a groundless rumour that Russian forces had crossed the demarcation lines laid down in the armistice, the British Cabinet resolved on 9 February to send ships to Constantinople and to invite all the neutral Powers to do the same. It was also decided that an international conference should be convened to resolve the territorial problems which had arisen during the crisis. Later, on the offer of Bismarck's services as 'honest broker', Berlin was chosen as the venue for the conference, which was to be glorified into a Congress.

In proud Palmerstonian and now Beaconsfieldian style, six British ironclad battleships left Besika Bay on 15 February, steamed through the Dardanelles and anchored in the Sea of Marmora; though the Sultan, fearful of the proximity of his Russian foe, had not dared to issue the *firman* officially authorising their passage. The Russians, however, had stopped well short of Constantinople. Nevertheless, Russia exacted a high price for her forbearance, in the form of a treaty signed with Turkey at San Stefano (near Constantinople) on 3 March. This provided for the complete independence of Balkan countries which were already virtually self-governing, and for cessions of territory to them; for the transfer of eastern Armenia to Russia, and the payment of a forty-five million pound indemnity to her; and, most strikingly, for the creation of a much enlarged Bulgaria which would be, in effect, a dependency of Russia. Russia, however, was prepared not to regard these terms as final but to submit them to the judgement of the international Congress.

The ending of the armed conflict and the decision to call the Congress were already large successes for Beaconsfield. He wanted to build on them in order to strengthen Britain in the Mediterranean. To this end he ordered 7,000 Indian troops to be sent to Malta through the Suez Canal – a striking demonstration of the unity of imperial interests, combining Indian defence with resistance to Russia in the Mediterranean. In May he obtained from Turkey the cession of Cyprus to Britain, and the assurance of safeguards for the Sultan's Christian subjects, in return for a defensive alliance against further Russian attack. 'Cyprus', he claimed in a letter to the Queen in May, 'is the key of Western Asia'. Its acquisition, together with the proposed defensive alliance, would strengthen both Britain's power in the eastern Mediterranean and her hold on India, and would make Turkey a much stronger barrier against Russia than she had been before the war. The whole policy would greatly enhance the supreme Beaconsfieldian object of 'welding together your Majesty's Indian Empire and Great Britain'.[25]

The British representatives at the Berlin Congress went there armed with the provisions of the Anglo–Russian Conventions, which proposed considerable reductions in the Russian gains in the Treaty of San Stefano. Beaconsfield, his health temporarily restored, accompanied Salisbury, who had replaced Derby as Foreign Secretary, to the Berlin assembly. They arrived on 11 June, a few days before the opening of the Congress. Proceedings lasted for a month. The main work of negotiating for the advancement of British interests fell to Salisbury. But the elderly premier was the biggest social success of the Congress. Many of the most powerful figures in Europe seemed suddenly to have become very Beaconsfield-conscious. His peculiar exotic background and multi-faceted fame ensured that he graduated at Berlin from being the cynosure of Britain to being the cynosure of Europe. Continental statesmen were even struggling to read his novels.

The Congress proceedings exhausted him. But this was largely because illness troubled him again at times and because he attended many functions which were, no doubt, socially enjoyable, but not essential – especially the dinner parties which had long been one of his favourite forms of entertainment. He scored political as well as social triumphs. Bismarck, the German Chancellor, was suspicious of him when the Congress began, especially because he had joined in a protest against a German threat of war with France in 1875. But the Chancellor warmed to him, no doubt recognising a kindred soul in diplomatic absorption, subtlety and mastery. He bestowed on Beaconsfield one of the most generous accolades that he ever received – 'Der alte Jude, das ist der Mann'.

In the Treaty of Berlin, signed at the end of the Congress on 13 July, the Anglo–Russian Conventions on the re-arrangement of the territorial provisions of San Stefano were generally confirmed. Contrary to popular myth, Beacons-field did not have to order a special train and threaten to leave on it in order to obtain agreement to additional conditions he wanted, though he did hint that he might have to break up the Congress.[26] In the Balkans, Rumania and Serbia became fully independent, Bosnia and Herzegovina were placed under Austro–Hungarian occupation, and the enlarged, independent Bulgaria was greatly reduced in size. In Armenia, the important seaport of Batum on the south-east shore of the Black Sea was annexed by Russia, but the towns of Ardahan, Kars and Bayazid, which Russia had also wanted to keep, were returned to Turkey after a good deal of wrangling over the precise line of the frontier.

The Berlin settlement was widely regarded as a victory in Beaconsfield's own country, whither he returned on 16 July. The acquisition of Cyprus, confirmed by the Congress, won particular applause. The premier could justly tell the welcoming crowd gathered in London that he had brought back 'peace with honour'. He capped his triumph by mod-estly declining the honours which the Queen offered to him and his relations, except the Garter which he accepted for himself and which was also, at his suggestion, bestowed on Salisbury.

It was at this moment, rather than in 1868 or 1874, that he reached the top of his pole. He had attained not only national (as in 1874) but European triumph. Some aspects of the Berlin settlement had proved hard to achieve, and some did not last very long. The conclusions on Bulgaria were altered in seven years, and even Cyprus did not retain its potential importance as a naval base after Egypt was occupied by British forces in 1882. But Beaconsfield's main object, the defence of Turkey as an aid to British imperial interests, particularly in regard to India, had been clearly attained. His personal success as a participant in the diplomatic discussions and the social festivities at Berlin, and the territorial conclusions reached there which were so much in his interests, represented his very peak of power. They were also accompanied by domestic political triumph. He had overcome the powerful challenge from Gladstone and his agitation, and the threat from divisions in his own Cabinet. Altogether it was difficult to imagine what further success he could hope to gain. But, as was not unusual with those who had attained great power and prestige, the future brought nothing but anti-climax.

.   .   .

DECLINE AND FALL, 1878–80

After its shining success at Berlin, Beaconsfield's Government decided not to seek another electoral mandate immediately. Although the situation was not clear-cut, the decision may have been mistaken, for thenceforth the Government sank under a weight of troubles and Gladstone was able to defeat it at the polls in April 1880. The troubles were both domestic and imperial. At home, economic recession in the mid- and late 1870s, after the long boom which had lasted since 1850 with scarcely a break, was bringing disillusion and discontent. Unemployment became quite high, rising to eleven per cent of the work-force in 1879. Depression was especially marked in agriculture, which, unlike industry, experienced a decline that lasted for many decades rather than being merely temporary.

The agricultural slump, caused by the much faster and easier rail and steamship methods of importing goods from abroad, had particularly sharp effects in Ireland, both social and political in nature. Social discontent resulting from economic depression united with the rising political force of the Home Rule party, which made its presence felt at Westminster through mastering the art of obstructing debates. Reform specifically for Ireland was one sphere of policy which Disraeli almost wholly, and short-sightedly, ignored during his ministry of 1874–80. Practically the only exception to this glaring absence was the introduction of a change in the university system in 1879, when the Royal University was formed as a general examining body for the various university colleges.[27]

In the realm of empire, too, ministers experienced some of their worst problems at the end of the 1870s. Ironically, the very sphere in which Beaconsfield had won his recent glowing victory was to prove his undoing. The failure of imperial plans and ventures which were an expensive charge on public funds stimulated Gladstone to fresh oratorical efforts and carried him to electoral victory.

Two imperial crises came to a head in 1878–9, one in the familiar sphere of Indian defence against Russia and the other in South Africa. In the first of these the independent buffer-state of Afghanistan was the theatre of action. The threat of Russian encroachment there in 1878 did not at first greatly concern Beaconsfield, and he desired no immediate step to be taken. But the Indian Viceroy, Lord Lytton, son of his old friend Bulwer Lytton, was making positive moves to secure the north-west frontier. He was alarmed by the steady advance of Russia in Turkestan, and by a growing intimacy between the Russian governor of that region and Sher Ali, Amir of Afghanistan. Lytton's efforts to advance British influence in Afghanistan were to no avail. Sher Ali, though he claimed British protection, became more deeply committed to Russia and showed hostility towards the British regime in India.

In July 1878 a Russian mission appeared at Kabul, the Afghan capital. Although Sher Ali had made a formal protest against the mission, he nevertheless welcomed it with full honours and signed some sort of agreement with its leader. For years Sher Ali had declined to receive a mission from the

Viceroy of India, whose protection he claimed. So, in view of the reception of the Russian mission, Lytton decided to send his own mission to Kabul, and to insist on its reception with due honours. He obtained the sanction of the India Office for this initiative. However, Beaconsfield considered that he was acting too hastily, in view of negotiations that were taking place with a Russia which seemed reasonably disposed to a conciliatory settlement of the issue. The premier and most of his Cabinet were also reluctant to support Lytton's desire for war with Afghanistan after the British mission was stopped by Sher Ali at the entrance to the Khyber Pass. But the British Government did decide on war after Sher Ali had ignored a cabinet demand for an apology and for the reception of a British resident minister in his country. Troops from India consequently advanced through the mountain passes into Afghanistan on 21 November 1878.

The Liberal Opposition leaders condemned the war policy, but it was supported by large majorities in both Houses of Parliament. The British invasion of Afghanistan was successful. Sher Ali fled to Russian Turkestan, but he obtained no help from the Tsar and died a few months later. His son Yakub Khan, the new Amir, signed a treaty in May 1879 accepting British control of his foreign policy and agreeing to receive a British mission and a British Resident at Kabul. But the Afghan turbulence was not yet finished. In early September news was received that the members of the British mission and the Resident, Sir Louis Cavagnari, had been attacked by Afghan insurgents and massacred. This proved, however, to be no permanent set-back to the assertion of British control. Sir Frederick Roberts launched a military attack on the uprising and crushed it. But there was still a recurrence of resistance, and a final settlement was left for the next Government to make in 1881. The regime of a new Amir was supported by Britain in exchange for control of his foreign relations.

The South African crisis had some strong similarities to the Afghan imbroglio – another venturesome and impatient British governor anxious for imperial advance, and a further disaster for British prestige before military victory was gained. Sir Bartle Frere, the new Governor of Cape Colony and High Commissioner for South Africa, arrived to take up his posts in 1877, at a time when it was decided to annex the Transvaal to the British possessions. The Zulus, under their king Cetewayo, felt threatened by this British advance, while Frere was determined to destroy Zulu independence as an obstacle to British expansion. Frere prepared for the war he wanted with the Zulus. He ignored clear instructions from home – sent by Hicks Beach, Carnarvon's successor as Colonial Secretary – that he should not engage in armed conflict; and he sent Cetewayo an ultimatum which it was practically impossible for that formidable monarch to accept. War commenced in January 1879, and on the twenty-second of that month occurred the famous Zulu victory at Isandhlwana, when a British force under Lord Chelmsford was practically wiped out.

A loud public outcry at home demanded the recall of Frere and Chelmsford, but the former, though officially censured for his disobedience and having his power greatly circumscribed, was allowed to continue in office in Cape Colony. Chelmsford retained his military command, advancing into Zululand and winning a decisive victory at Ulundi on 4 July 1879. After this, his reputation partly rehabilitated, he had the wisdom to resign.

Another success for the Government in Africa was the establishment of dual control over Egypt by Britain and France in June. The Zulu affair, however, had made Beaconsfield indecisive, angry and ill. He had prevaricated when he should have been resolute, and had acted petulantly when things went awry instead of exhibiting his usual impassivity. Perhaps it was beginning to seem that it was time for him to resign.[28]

.   .   .

The forward movements in Afghanistan and Zululand were both eventually successful, but were both expensive in money, lives and effort. Both exhibited the depressing drawbacks of imperialism, as well as – after a time – some of its glamour. At a time of commercial recession there were naturally widespread complaints about the exorbitant cost, unaccompanied by immediate glowing victory but rather by the reverse. Gladstone, the scourge of monetary waste, of imperial *coups*, and of Beaconsfield, was fully ready to exploit the situation. He seized his opportunity in a fashion now expected of him. His Midlothian campaign of vigorous denunciation from 24 November to 8 December 1879 – delivered in the area where he had been adopted as a candidate in the next election – assailed not only recent colonial policy but the whole record of the Government. Beaconsfield, ill and frail, and in any case no match for Gladstone in outdoor oratory, made no comparable reply.

A Liberal election victory, however, seemed by no means assured. Despite their early expensive failures, both the Afghan and the Zulu wars had been successful by the end of 1879. There were some encouraging signs of economic revival. At the beginning of 1880 the Cabinet did not plan an early dissolution. Ministers seemed prepared to stay in office, perhaps for another session. In February, however, two Conservative by-election successes greatly promoted thoughts of an early dissolution.

On 6 March 1880 the Cabinet decided to dissolve Parliament and hold a general election. The dissolution was announced in Parliament on 8 March, to the surprise of both Conservatives and Liberals. Beaconsfield decided to campaign mainly against the demand for Irish Home Rule. His election manifesto was in the form of a letter on 9 March to the Lord Lieutenant of Ireland, the Duke of Marlborough, in which he said that 'men of light and leading' would resist the 'destructive doctrine' of Home Rule. His biographer G.E. Buckle said of the letter: 'with the exception of the characteristically Disraelian phrase, "men of light and leading", this was not a very happily worded document'. But the very phrase 'men of light and leading' was singled out for criticism by political opponents as being ungrammatical.[29] Altogether it was an inauspicious start. The Government might have been hoping to obtain the support of some Irish Catholic immigrant voters in Great Britain because of their support for denominational schools. But no such elector who sympathised with Home Rule was at all likely to support Beaconsfield after the issue of his manifesto. Instead, 'vote against Benjamin Disraeli as you should vote against the mortal enemy of your country and your race' was the message put out by the Home Rule Confederation of Great Britain.[30]

The Liberals easily had the best of the oratorical contest

during the election. Gladstone conducted a second Midlothian campaign in the latter half of March. Beaconsfield, Salisbury, Cairns and others among the Conservative leadership could not reply in the same form since peers were not allowed to make election speeches. Among Conservatives who were not thus hampered, the oratorical effectiveness of Northcote, Cross and Hicks Beach could not match that of Hartington, Bright and Harcourt on the other side. Even the Conservative party organisation, which had performed effectively in the 1874 contest, had run into decline and could not rival the efficient if divisive National Liberal Federation, established in 1877.[31]

The Liberals, so divided in 1874 that they allowed their opponents to be returned, had pulled together more effectively for the 1880 election. Nevertheless, the extent of the Liberal victory was probably unexpected by both parties. The Conservative Central Office had anticipated a reduced, but still a working, majority for its own side. But the result of the first day's polling on 31 March was enough to place such a hope in jeopardy. By 3 April the Conservatives had lost fifty seats, and had no hope of a majority. The final result showed that the relative number of seats held by the two main parties in the old Parliament was almost exactly reversed, the Liberals now being over a hundred ahead of the Conservatives, 353 to 238. The Home Rulers increased their seats to sixty-one, so the Liberals' overall majority was only slightly greater than the Conservatives' in 1874.[32]

The Cabinet decided on 15 April that they would resign without waiting for the new Parliament to meet. Beaconsfield, after dealing with necessary business (and outraging the ritualists once again by appointing the well-known evangelical Canon J.C. Ryle as the first Anglican Bishop of Liverpool), relinquished office on 21 April. The Queen, after taking Beaconsfield's advice, reluctantly appointed his great rival, 'the People's William', as her Prime Minister for the second time. He had won the current round in their continuing struggle, and, on account of Beaconsfield's death a year later, there was not to be another round on the same scale. Disraeli's triumph over Gladstone in 1867 had been followed by Gladstone's victory at the polls in 1868. Similarly, Beaconsfield's defeat of Gladstone over foreign policy in 1877–8 had been succeeded by Gladstone's election victory in 1880. Beaconsfield had not been successful in displacing the Liberals as a party with a continuing majority. The Conservatives had still only gained one majority since 1841, and the Liberals had gained seven. After his largely impressive ministry of six years, Beaconsfield had to accept the role of Opposition for his party once more.

. . .

OPPOSITION AGAIN, 1880–1

Lord Beaconsfield lived for exactly a year after his resignation. He was plagued by illness, especially gout, but until the last fortnight of his life he gave no indication that he was about to sink into his grave. He remained, indeed, remarkably active for one of his age and infirmity. He was Conservative leader in the House of Lords, responsible for Opposition policy in that House, and he told a meeting of 500 Conservative politicians on 19 May that he would continue as party leader. Until his death he remained the unchallenged party chieftain – more remote but more eminent than he had ever been before. After his electoral defeat of 1868 some restlessness and outright disillusion had developed against his leadership, but it was unthinkable that such feelings should be directed against the hero of Berlin, in spite of his later experience of anti-climax and a further electoral defeat. Until the sudden physical decline which led to his death it was quite possible that he would survive to lead his party against Gladstone in the next general election, and even succeed him as Prime Minister.

Apart from his continuing political interests and activity, he remained an enthusiastic letter-writer. He sent twenty-two letters to the Queen during his last year, and maintained his frequent correspondence with Ladies Bradford and Chesterfield. To these and other correspondents he described Gladstone as 'the A.V.' (Arch-Villain).[33] He also continued to be a frequent attender at dinner parties where he would appear sometimes bright and sharp in conversation, sometimes silent and decrepit. Many people on such occasions wanted to talk to the amiable old celebrity, but, although usually participating with enjoyment, he would preserve his habitual semi-detachment, alert and watchful for the slightest bit of gossip which might be of political, social or fictional use.

He also completed and published his last novel, *Endymion*. More than half of this had been written many years before, between the time that *Lothair* was published in 1870 and his return to office in 1874. Most of the remainder was probably written in the late summer and autumn of 1878, and the work was finished in the summer of 1880. Before publication in November, T. Norton Longman agreed to pay the fabulous sum of £10,000 for all rights in the novel – probably the largest amount paid for any book up to that time. Sales of the first edition, however, were not as great as *Lothair*, and Beaconsfield generously offered to return £3,000 in exchange for receiving agreed royalties on copies sold in the future. But Longman declined to accept, and, through the aid of a cheaper edition, all expenses on the book had been recouped by April 1881.[34]

Now forgotten like most of Disraeli's novels, *Endymion* is another fairy-tale aristocratic romance. It has the merit of being rather more readable than most of his fiction; also like most of his novels, it casts many political and social sidelights. But it has nothing of the serious social purpose of *Sybil* and *Coningsby*. The hero, Endymion Ferrars, insipid as Lothair, is a dull if charming nonentity who rises to become Prime Minister simply through 'being there' and benefiting from the determined efforts of much abler relatives and friends on his behalf. Apart from both of them having attained the premiership, it is difficult to imagine a greater contrast between the author and his central character.

Endymion contains portraits and slight touches of many of the great and famous people whom Beaconsfield had encountered. These included both Bismarck and Manning. The latter was given much more favourable treatment than in *Lothair*, no doubt because considerations of educational policy had caused him to revert to being pro-Conservative. But there was no portrait of Gladstone. This absorbing undertaking was left for the next novel, which the old ex-premier began to write with his usual zest fifty-five years after he had composed *Vivian Grey*. Nine short chapters and a few additional lines of the untitled novel were written before his death, and were published first in *The Times* (in three instalments) in January 1905 and then as an appendix to the fifth volume of Monypenny and Buckle.[35] The work primarily concerns one Joseph Toplady Falconet, who:

> had been a child of singular precocity. His power of acquisition was remarkable, and, as he advanced in youth, his talents were evidently not merely those which ripen before their time. He was a grave boy, and scarcely ever known to smile; and this not so much from a want of sympathy for those among whom he was born and bred, for he seemed far from being incapable of domestic affection, but rather from a complete deficiency in the sense of humour, of which he seemed quite debarred. His memory was vigorous, ready, and retentive; but his chief peculiarity was his disputatious temper, and the flow of language which, even as a child, was ever at command to express his arguments.
>
> . . . Firm in his faith in an age of dissolving creeds, he wished to believe that he was the man ordained to vindicate the sublime cause of religious truth. With these ardent hopes, he had renounced the suggestion which he had once favoured of taking Orders. It was as the lay champion of the Church that he desired to act, and believed that in such a position his influence would be infinitely greater than in that of a clergyman whatever his repute.[36]

This was unmistakably the rival with whom the author had been locked in repeated combats, sometimes resulting in his triumph and sometimes his fall. Unfortunately the work is not long enough to develop more than the beginnings of a parliamentary and social life for Joseph Toplady Falconet. The failure to complete and publish the novel prevents us from seeing how such a work would have reacted on the political fortunes of the author and of the model for his main character.

A good deal more of Beaconsfield's attention was given to politics than to writing fiction or attending social occasions during his last year. Though he lived mainly at Hughenden during the summer and autumn of 1880, he had to be in London for debates in the Lords and party meetings. As he was without a town house until the beginning of 1881, he was glad to reside in a suite of rooms placed at his disposal by Alfred de Rothschild, second son of his friend Baron Lionel de Rothschild. From January 1881 he leased for nine years – 'that, I think, will see me out', he told a friend[37] – a house in a part of London he greatly liked, at 19, Curzon Street, Mayfair, close to Hyde Park which he had overlooked for so long when living at Grosvenor Gate.

Beaconsfield gladly noted the embarrassed state of the new Government in trying to cope with the intense difficulties which immediately beset it, including Irish economic, social and political problems, the Bradlaugh case, and (an ironic touch, in view of the Conservatives' recent embarrassments) imperial disputes and set-backs. But it seemed clear to him that the Opposition would not win widespread confidence if it incited and encouraged 'the party of revolution', by which he meant some hundred (as he estimated) radical MPs who were allegedly trying to destroy the aristocratic order, the monarchy, and the established Churches. The Government should be supported against such extravagant objects, but not if it misguidedly tried to make concessions to them. He claimed that Gladstone was consorting with Fenians and revolutionaries, and that the Whig peers in the ministry were not standing up sufficiently for the interests of their own class. 'I really think the country is going to the devil', he told Selina Bradford on 7 July 1880;[38] and on 28 November he told her:

> The Whig element dare not say Boo to a goose – much less to Gladstone, who certainly [is] not a goose. He is now really the head of the Radicals, and sets the Whigs at defiance.[39]

In 1880 Beaconsfield and his party supported Whigs and other moderate Liberals against one of the ministry's Irish measures, the Compensation for Disturbance Bill which would have temporarily prohibited Irish landlords from evicting without compensation tenants who failed to pay their rent. This bill, which was opposed on the grounds that its provisions seriously infringed the rights of landed proprietors and might be extended later to Great Britain, aroused the resistance of many Liberals. Twenty Liberal MPs voted against the second reading in the Commons, and fifty abstained, the reading being carried by 299 votes to 217. Lord Lansdowne, who had a large amount of land in Ireland and gave sympathetic treatment to his tenants, left the Government on this issue. In the Lords the bill was trounced by 282 to 51, more Liberals voting against than in favour. On any grounds of objective justice, the bill should have been carried in view of the deep and widespread poverty currently afflicting rural Ireland. But defence of private property rights carried the day, championed by Beaconsfield against any calls for sympathy with the destitute Irish peasant.

Lord Blake has said that the ex-premier was, at heart, wholly out of sympathy with Irish radicals, and that 'in terms of political tactics in 1880 his resistance to the Bill was shrewd enough'.[40] Certainly Beaconsfield had shown a remarkable and momentous lapse in his usual realism by offering hardly any reforms of distinctively Irish problems during his recent ministry. But he retained his fundamentally realistic approach nonetheless; and if he were to win power again and was confronted with more immediate Irish matters than the assumed need to resist 'revolutionary forces', he would be likely to turn his fertile political skill to evolving and introducing measures of Irish reform. His resistance to the bill certainly conformed with his political tactics in 1880, which were to support the Whigs against 'the party of revolution', and divide the Liberals by this means just as he had divided them in 1867 by encouraging the radicals. But in different circumstances political tactics might dictate the adoption or encouragement of measures which appealed to the Home Rulers and land reformers.

Early in 1881 Beaconsfield supported in the Lords the Government's 'coercion' bill (or Bill for the Protection of Persons and Property in Ireland) which was easily carried. On other matters, he took a strong line in imperial defence by speaking on 9 March 1881 against the evacuation of Kandahar in Afghanistan, demonstrating again his determination to protect the Indian empire. The speech, though not among his most powerful orations, was perhaps his most striking effort in this latter period. In the course of it he had a dig at the now Liberal Derby, who had spoken animatedly against retaining Kandahar, by saying: 'I do not know that there is anything that would excite enthusiasm in him except when he contemplates the surrender of some national possession'.[41] He was careful, however, not to make his party appear so rigid or so careless of the opinions of some of its own followers that it might try to reject a Game Bill, an Employers' Liability Bill, or a Burials Bill in 1880.

The possibility of Conservative disunity seems to have been of some concern to him because of the emergence of a ginger-group in the Commons known as 'the fourth party'. This included John Gorst, Drummond Wolff, Lord Randolph Churchill, and sometimes A.J. Balfour. The 'party' was determined to be the scourge of Gladstone even at the cost of embarrassing its own front bench, led by Sir Stafford Northcote whom it considered unduly mild in spite of his efficiency. Beaconsfield derived some sympathy with their aims and feelings from his own past experience. On the other hand, he had no wish to embarrass Northcote, whose skill as leader he respected.[42] He wrote to Drummond Wolff:

I fully appreciate your feelings and those of your friends, but you must stick to Northcote. He represents the respectability of the party. I wholly sympathise with you all, because I was never respectable myself.... Don't on any account break with Northcote, but defer to him as often as you can.[43]

.   .   .

Beaconsfield made his last appearance and his last speech in the Lords on 15 March 1881, when he supported a Vote of Condolence to the Queen on the assassination of Tsar Alexander II. Even the antagonism between Russia and Britain in the 1870s, and the tensions persisting into the 1880s, could be minimised in these circumstances, when the ex-premier described Alexander as 'the most eminent prince that ever filled the throne of Russia'.[44]

After this, a physique already undermined by recent illness could not hold out much longer against the fierce effects of the hardest winter for many years, stretching into a cold March and April. He had written to Selina in November: 'I cannot use my legs.... I have never had a fit of gout like it. It has attacked me with renovating ferocity. It reminds me of poor Lord Derby.'[45] The gout continued to menace him, though asthma was currently much less of a problem. In March he was relentlessly attending dinner parties, but on the twenty-third of that month he succumbed to a chill and never left his Curzon Street house (and scarcely his bed or couch) again. He was surrounded by medical attention, received many expressions of both royal and popular concern, and was visited by many friends and acquaintances (including Gladstone). At one stage he was showing some signs of recovery. But these did not last, and after them he grew steadily worse. On 19 April he breathed his last.

He died not only full of years, honour and acclaim, and (until a few weeks before his death) actively leading his party, but – for one who had been subject to great and growing debt for forty years – full of wealth as well. He still had a mortgage of £57,000 on Hughenden (representing the amount which his debts had reached by 1862), but his resources had grown greatly through fortunate legacies and large sums received from his novels, and through considerably enlarging the Hughenden estate. His will was eventually proved at £84,000 – a great deal more than the amount of his mortgage.

.   .   .

NOTES

1. Quoted G.I.T. Machin, *Politics and the Churches in Great Britain, 1869 to 1921*, Oxford 1987, p. 69.
2. R. Blake, *Disraeli*, London 1966, p. 543; P. Smith, *Disraelian Conservatism and Social Reform*, London 1967, p. 199.
3. Machin, *Politics and the Churches, 1869 to 1921*, pp. 87–94.
4. Ibid., pp. 70–86; R.W. Davis, *Disraeli*, London 1976, pp. 180–1; J. Bentley, *Ritualism and Politics in Victorian Britain: the attempt to legislate for belief*, Oxford 1978, p. 46ff.
5. For a detailed account of the reforms see Smith, *Disraelian Conservatism and Social Reform*, pp. 198–265, 277–8, 299–301; and cf. Davis, *Disraeli*, pp. 174–8.
6. V. Skretkowicz (ed.), *Florence Nightingale's Notes on Nursing*, revised with additions, London 1992, p. 101.
7. Smith, *Disraelian Conservatism and Social Reform*, p. 217.
8. For the important Liberal contribution to the measures, see J. Spain, 'Trade unionists, Gladstonian Liberals and the labour law reforms of 1875', in E.F. Biagini and A.J. Reid (eds), *Currents of Radicalism: popular radicalism,*

organised labour and party politics in Britain, 1850–1914, Cambridge 1991, pp. 109–33, especially pp. 128–31.

9. Blake, *Disraeli*, p. 554; Smith, *Disraelian Conservatism and Social Reform*, pp. 289–90.

10. Quoted in W.F. Monypenny and G.E. Buckle, *The Life of Benjamin Disraeli, Earl of Beaconsfield*, 6 vols, London 1910–20, vol. V, p. 483 (hereafter cited as Monypenny & Buckle).

11. Quoted in Blake, *Disraeli*, p. 564.

12. Cf. C.C. Eldridge, *England's Mission: the imperial idea in the age of Gladstone and Disraeli, 1868–80*, London 1973, pp. 180–1.

13. Quoted in Blake, *Disraeli*, p. 584; cf. Monypenny & Buckle, vol. V, pp. 439–52, 460–1.

14. Quoted in Blake, *Disraeli*, pp. 584–5.

15. Quoted in ibid., p. 581.

16. Monypenny & Buckle, vol. V, pp. 427–32, 456–71; Blake, *Disraeli*, pp. 562–4.

17. Accounts of the whole episode in Monypenny & Buckle, vol. VI, pp. 1–368; Blake, *Disraeli*, pp. 575–654; R. Shannon, *The Age of Disraeli, 1868–81: the rise of Tory democracy*, London 1992, pp. 273–307.

18. Shannon, *The Age of Disraeli*, p. 276.

19. Quoted in ibid., pp. 281–2.

20. Beaconsfield to Derby, 25 September 1876; Monypenny & Buckle, vol. VI, p. 104.

21. *Tancred, or the new Crusade* (The Bradenham Edition of the Novels and Tales of Benjamin Disraeli, first Earl of Beaconsfield, 12 vols, vol. X, London 1927), p. 358.

22. Quoted in Monypenny & Buckle, vol. VI, p. 60.

23. 3 October 1877; quoted in ibid., pp. 180–1.

24. Quoted in ibid., p. 90.

25. 5 May 1878; quoted in ibid., p. 291.

26. Blake, *Disraeli*, p. 648.

27. T.W. Moody, 'The Irish university question in the nineteenth century', *History*, vol. XLIII, 1958, pp. 101–2.

28. Monypenny & Buckle, vol. VI, pp. 369–404, 478–85; Blake, *Disraeli*, pp. 657–74.

29. Machin, *Politics and the Churches, 1869 to 1921*, p. 114.

30. Quoted in Monypenny & Buckle, vol. VI, p. 516.

31. Ibid., p. 519; Blake, *Disraeli*, pp. 704–5; Smith, *Disraelian Conservatism and Social Reform*, pp. 309–17; Shannon, *The*

Age of Disraeli, pp. 369–83; T. Lloyd, *The General Election of 1880*, Oxford 1968, pp. 63–89.

32. Blake, *Disraeli*, pp. 711–12; Lloyd, *General Election*, pp. 134–60.
33. Monypenny & Buckle, vol. VI, pp. 541–4.
34. Ibid., pp. 551–4, 568–70.
35. Monypenny & Buckle, vol. V, pp. 531–60.
36. Ibid., pp. 533–5.
37. Janetta Manners, Duchess of Rutland, *Some Personal Recollections of the Earl of Beaconsfield, K.G.*, Edinburgh 1881, pp. 27–8.
38. Monypenny & Buckle, vol. VI, pp. 580–2.
39. Ibid., p. 593.
40. Blake *Disraeli*, p. 728.
41. Monypenny & Buckle, vol. VI, p. 603.
42. Ibid., p. 607.
43. Quoted in ibid., p. 589. Cf. Shannon, *The Age of Disraeli*, pp. 388–93.
44. Monypenny & Buckle, vol. VI, p. 608.
45. Quoted in ibid., p. 592.

CONCLUSIONS

In considering Disraeli in relation to power and the use he made of it, the most striking factor is his personal determination to overcome all obstacles and rise as far as possible in politics. In spite of his persistent dedication to writing novels, it first became clear when he was little beyond twenty that he had a great interest in politics and would try to get a footing in them by winning a seat in Parliament.

In pursuing this aim he had little assistance from his background. He was neither aristocratic nor very rich, nor did he have a conventional upper-class education. His religion would have ruled out parliamentary aspirations if he had not, quite fortuitously, been baptised as a Christian. Having received this essential attribute for entry to Parliament he could try his luck in getting elected like any other talented, moderately wealthy and moderately educated male scion of the middle classes. He could pursue all means to this end such as exhibiting his oratorical and journalistic powers, cultivating high society, and especially seeking the patronage or sponsorship of a powerful party leader who would give him the political support and encouragement which he did not naturally receive from his own family background.

What was particularly needed in his ambition to enter Parliament – especially in view of his lack of conventional educational openings and the social set-backs which he largely brought on himself – was firm and sustained will-power. This was one of Disraeli's leading characteristics and it had to be employed continuously, not only in getting elected to Parliament in the first place, but thenceforth in carrying him through lengthy vicissitudes which lasted for

nearly forty years before he at length obtained a parliamentary majority. The encouragement he received from
the passing of the first Reform Act was not translated
into success until he had stood persistently in elections and
transformed his prospects by obtaining the firm support of a
leading Conservative, Lord Lyndhurst. After he entered the
Commons he had to overcome the frustration he received
from his party leader – which he did by overthrowing that
leader. He then had to do all he could to extend and support
his truncated party, giving it new progressive policies which
were very similar to, and went considerably beyond, those
of the defeated Peel. The long arid period from 1846 to
1874, when he was usually in Opposition, was broken by
the encouragement obtained from periods of office and
from the very occasional parliamentary triumph, notably the
Second Reform Act. Without these oases amidst a generally
desert-like political existence even Disraeli's will might have
weakened, and he might not have survived as a leader long
enough to obtain his majority in 1874.

The ministry which began in 1874 was very successful until
1878, and he rose to greater heights when, as the leader of
the great isolated Power, he broke into the highest counsels
of Europe, and moderated and controlled that continent's
destinies as they were debated and decided at the Congress
of Berlin. A triumphant political and social success at home,
he proved to be the same abroad, the centre of attention and
the successful arbiter at a great and sparkling international
gathering hosted by his new-found admirer, Count Bismarck.
After Berlin his luck did not hold. His political success
disintegrated for a variety of reasons, and he was unexpectedly
and mortifyingly defeated again by his old, familiar rival in
1880. Thereafter circumstances prevented him from doing
much about reviving his ambitions of a further electoral
success, though he did achieve some triumph over Gladstone's
second ministry and was able to revel in its embarrassments.

. . .

Apart from his determination to rise to power and to
exploit every opportunity provided by party and policy to
do so, other political considerations in Disraeli's career were

of secondary importance. He was completely without any ideological preconceptions which might have made loyal service to ideals a more compelling demand than even rising to a powerful position. To Disraeli, the prospect of gaining power was always superior to any demand to vindicate ideals or to maintain loyalty to leaders.

It is, indeed, difficult to say what ideals he had. He did have, of necessity, a definite attachment to a major party, without which he could not have attempted to gain power at all. But he could have gone into either of the main parties. In his youth he was a Canningite or 'liberal Tory'. When he was rather older he became a radical and stood in several elections in this capacity – though he was far from attaching himself to any radical coterie or school of thought, and maintained a flexible and interested independence. He claimed to be anti-Whig, but he had few anti-Whig principles or policies. If he could have found a powerful and reliable patron in the Liberal party, such as Lord Durham, this posture would doubtless have been modified and perhaps abandoned. Instead of this he was drawn again by chance into the Conservative party when his mistress introduced him to the all-important prominent party figure who could give him some of the vital support he needed.

Disraeli was always a Conservative thereafter. But he experienced ironic revivals of his radical past when he sought to make use of Liberal divisions in order to gain radical support for his own policies and party prospects – as he tried to do unsuccessfully over his budget of 1852 and successfully over his Reform Bill in 1867. Loyalty to the party leadership was subordinated to his own determination to rise. Peel's short-sighted decision not to give him office in 1841 reaped a whirlwind in Disraeli's growing frustration and hostility and his central part in that statesman's downfall in 1846. There was subtle justice in the fact that Peel did not fall directly over Protection – to which Disraeli was probably only loosely attached – but over his Irish 'coercion' policy in which Disraeli would probably have supported him if he had not been determined to bring him down.

Both before and after 1846 (more obviously after, because of his temporary espousal of ultra-Toryism in 1845–6) Disraeli showed that he was ready to fit into, indeed to help in leading, the general liberalism which now guided the policies of both parties. He (like Gladstone) had been a Canningite when the liberal trend in government policy took root in the 1820s, so it could be said that he was in at the liberal beginning in the nineteenth century. He largely maintained a liberal approach thereafter. Though he defended Protection and landed aristocratic interests against Peel, he had also made public statements of admiration for the energy and economic strength of the middle classes. As well as the financial and commercial elements in his background which gave him some understanding and sympathy with the mercantile, manufacturing and financial middle class, he had probably derived some knowledge of Nonconformity from his attendance at a Unitarian school, and he seems to have had friendly feelings towards John Bright.

After 1846 realistic appraisal of the situation indicated that Protection should be abandoned, though financial compensation for agriculture should be obtained in return and support for the landed interest – essential for any Conservative leader to maintain – preserved in this and other ways. During the rest of his career he helped to carry through many liberal, reforming policies while never abandoning what was for him a politic but also a genuine desire to maintain the interests of the aristocracy.

. . .

Also subordinate to his overriding desire to gain and maintain power were the detailed policies he adopted. Disraeli never took up and pursued a policy which might not aid his political interest. His early opposition to the Poor Law and sympathy with Chartism were respectable Conservative attitudes at that time (though they did not endear him to Peel), but they were not so for much longer and he did not sustain them. He had a genuine desire to improve social conditions for the working class, but he did not urge this cause in any consistent or campaigning fashion, maintain it if it went clearly against aristocratic economic interests, or concern himself with its practical details. The ministries of 1866–8 and 1874–80 passed many significant social reforms, but Disraeli gave a benevolent and encouraging face to them rather than initiating or planning any of them himself. At these times he did not seem anxious to press particular reforms which he had advocated earlier and which were still unrealised. Social reforms were desirable to him, especially when they were likely to enlarge his political support, but he would not urge them if they were politically inappropriate to his party ends.

Parliamentary reform was undoubtedly less a matter of principle than social reform to Disraeli, but he urged parliamentary reform with more consistency and gave more time to it for much of his political life. For twenty years, from 1848 to 1868, he seems to have regarded electoral extension, adapted to his party's interest, as the most promising means of increasing that party's support and assisting it to gain a majority. He was helped in his objective by the Liberal divisions on the question. When at length he succeeded in carrying Reform Bills and their associated measures in 1867–8, he did so decidedly in his party interest but also by means of winning the support of radicals on the opposite benches. Moreover, he gained in the process the additional satisfaction of humiliating and defeating Gladstone. It was an exceedingly adroit performance, though it did not realise its objective of gaining a majority: Disraeli had to wait for Liberal disintegration and the strengthening of his party to give this to him in 1874. Parliamentary reform was of no further use to him after 1868. Like other policies, it was dropped when it no longer aided his political purpose. The secret ballot, introduced by Gladstone's ministry in 1872, was likely to undermine Conservative landed interests. Conservative interests would also be threatened by the move to extend household suffrage from the boroughs to the counties. Such an extension would enfranchise rural workers who might well vote against their landlord's wishes and transfer Conservative county seats to the Liberals. The prospect of parliamentary reform, on a careful and selective basis, assisted Disraeli's political aims for twenty years before 1868, but not for his remaining thirteen years after that.

Disraeli also subordinated economic policy to his political interests. He defended Protection in the mid-1840s against Peel's 'betrayal' of it, but he had only recently espoused a strong Protectionist line after previously supporting Peel's commercial changes. He took to defending Protection as his relations with Peel grew more bitter and the possibility of office in Peel's Government seemed to get further and further away. He might have convinced himself at the time that Protection was the right policy, but he soon afterwards gave it up, seeking to persuade his Protectionist party to follow him. To him, Protection had become politically redundant, though he wished to give substantial financial compensation to the landlords. After the 1852 election Protection was dropped by his party – an indication of the way in which that party (or much of it) adopted Peel's liberal policies after it had jettisoned Peel. The abandonment of Protection, however, was not necessarily final. Disraeli would no doubt have been prepared to take it up again if there had been a powerful demand from his party for it. But, although there was some demand for the revival of Protection by the late 1870s on account of commercial deterioration, the matter was not very strongly pressed before his death.

Defence of Britain's imperial interests seemed to be central to Conservative party objects. Disraeli's complaints about the burden of the colonies in 1852 and 1866 – 'a millstone round our necks', 'deadweights which we do not govern' – should be seen as irritated and isolated remarks of a Chancellor of the Exchequer subject to a multitude of demands for expenditure, rather than as indications of any consistent opposition to the maintenance of an empire. He was content to see self-government adopted in the settled colonies such as Canada, provided that this meant a reduction in British expenditure. But he wished nevertheless to maintain firm imperial links with these self-governing colonies, and well before his two 'imperial' speeches of 1872 he stressed the need to uphold the Empire. He laid particular emphasis on the prestige and commercial benefit to be obtained from maintaining the Indian section of the Empire and consolidating its links with Britain. His personal interest in the Orient and his acquaintance with the eastern Mediterranean region in which the Suez Canal – the new channel to India – was constructed, lent special emphasis to his concern with Britain's empire of the East. In spite of the embarrassments which excessively repressive action in his favoured Turkey caused him in the mid-1870s, he was a natural opponent of both Russia and Gladstone in the policy he espoused, which he was able substantially to vindicate at the Congress of Berlin.

For all his desire to consolidate the links with India, however, it cannot be assumed that he would have opposed self-government for India, in contrast to his acceptance of it in the white-settled colonies. Indian self-government did not become an issue during his lifetime, but there is no reason to think that he would have rejected it provided he thought it would strengthen the Empire. His advocacy, at the time of the Indian mutiny, of recognising and tolerating Indian culture, indicated the flexibility he was prepared to adopt in such questions as in so much else.

In religious matters and ecclesiastical disputes Disraeli was disposed to be tolerant, as was natural for one who was fundamentally apart from them. His main religious interest, at least for part of his life, lay in the possibility of reconciling the Jewish and Christian religions. Among British politicians this preoccupation was unique, and his arguments aroused very little sympathy. When he did show intolerance, as in opposing the Maynooth grant in 1845 or supporting the Public Worship Regulation Bill in 1874, he allowed political interest and pressure to prevail over his tolerant impulses. Similarly, for the sake of expected political advantage he upheld established Church privilege at one time, as in the early 1860s when he vigorously defended church rates, but relinquished it at another, as in the later 1860s when he agreed to the abolition of compulsory church rates.

In all aspects of his policy, therefore, the furthering of his party and of his own political fortunes was paramount. He had a genuine wish to carry certain reforms, but only if and when they assisted his political objectives. The desire for reform would not be allowed to conflict with political aspirations, but would only be applied when it assisted them.

. . .

Disraeli is a great and central figure in the history of the Conservative party. He revived its fortunes, even if he had first destroyed them. He spent long and arduous years in Opposition or minority Government, initiating policies, exploiting divisions and weaknesses among his opponents, and at times encouraging new methods of party organisation, until he gained a majority and became more influential than ever before. His memory was perpetuated not least in the form of the Primrose League, a large and popular Conservative organisation named after his favourite flower. Even today he is recalled as one of the chief founders of modern Conservative success and achievement, ironically accompanying Peel as a harbinger of the adaptability and flexibility which produced the sustained confidence and success of British Conservatism in the twentieth century.

The adulation with which present-day Conservatives regard him, however, is tempered and modulated by their particular view of policy. From this point of view, an opinion of Disraeli is almost invariably assumed from one or other of the vantage-points thrown up by contemporary political controversy rather than from cool and informed historical examination. Consequently, Disraeli tends to be seen today as an interventionist social reformer, a proto-Macmillan who was a precursor of the Welfare State, and is definitely not popular with Thatcherites. This view reflects the great current importance of social welfare questions and the different approaches taken towards them. On the other hand the era of imperial vindication and glorification which Disraeli helped to sustain is largely forgotten, and if Thatcherites concentrated on this they would probably have a far more favourable opinion of him. The Falklands campaign of 1982 was in a direct line of ancestry from the purchase of the Suez Canal shares and the despatch of a fleet through the Dardanelles.

Opinions of Disraeli which are assumed so confidently on the basis of so little knowledge of evidence cannot be regarded as historically valid. A proper assessment of Disraeli cannot be made from the attitudes, assumptions and controversies of the present day. He can only be convincingly assessed from a detailed study of his policies and attitudes in the context of his own time. For example, it cannot be assumed, from the limited social reforms of Disraeli's Governments in 1868 and 1874–6, that he would have approved of the Welfare State founded after 1945. Nor can it be assumed that the champion of imperialism in the 1870s would have opposed the dismantling of empire in the period 1945–70. Disraeli was both notably realistic and notably flexible, so it is quite possible that he would have accepted, indeed inaugurated, the end of empire and something resembling the Welfare State. But it is beyond the bounds of historical activity to make assumptions of this kind. It is also possible, if less likely, that he would have strongly resisted a Welfare State on the grounds of individualism and put up a determined fight against the loss of colonies. Therefore it is best to discount half-baked views of Disraeli which are reached mainly from present-day positions, and to limit one's assessment to the attitudes, policies and deeds of the man in his own time.

Disraeli died only a few years before a major change in British party politics, and one or two speculative thoughts may be hazarded on the effect he might have had on Conservatism if he had lived twenty years or so longer. Although he had shown no great interest in the territorial aspects of imperial expansion, he would probably have been quite at home as a leader of the imperialist wave which stretched from his own exploits in the 1870s to the early twentieth century. He would probably have reached the same conclusions as Salisbury did over the need to accept compromise, for the sake of party interests, in the electoral reforms of 1884 and 1885 – even though these changes were a further blow to the influence of the aristocracy. Under his continued leadership his party, when in power, might well have passed more social reforms than the Conservative and Unionist Governments in the 1880s and 1890s actually did. Apart from any genuine desire he had for such reforms, he would have seen them as a potential means of boosting support for the Conservative party, especially from the increasingly powerful working-class electors. It cannot be assumed, however, that he would have disapproved of the formation of a separate Labour party, as he would have seen this as having potentially weakening effects on the Liberal party.

It would seem likely that the crisis over Irish Home Rule in 1885 would have brought out all his gifts of political percipience and of swift and flexible action. He had almost entirely, and certainly mistakenly, ignored the question of reforms specifically for Ireland during his ministry of 1874–80, but he could not have ignored this question in the mid-1880s. His political adaptability, skill and influence might have caused him to go further, more successfully, than Lord Carnarvon (then Lord Lieutenant of Ireland,

and proponent of limited Irish self-government); and to have persuaded his colleagues, or most of them, to accept a Conservative plan of Home Rule which could have reassured Ulster. He might thus have been able to satisfy Gladstone's desire that the Conservatives would adopt Home Rule and carry it by means of their majority in the Lords. Such a solution would not have conflicted with his imperial interests, because these included the extension of self-government provided that imperial ties were maintained.

. . .

Consideration of Disraeli in the general context of British historical development leads one to give him a firm place in the liberal tendency which has marked politics and government (with variations) from the 1820s to the present day. This tendency was shaped and strengthened not only by Grey, Russell and Gladstone (who represented the Liberal section of liberalism), but also by Canning, Peel and Disraeli, who formed a Conservative section, initiating liberal reforms themselves and adapting to those passed by the Liberals. The Reform Act of 1832 endorsed and strengthened the liberal trend commenced by Canning and others in the 1820s, and indeed harking back to the pre-Revolution Pitt the Younger. The Act of 1832 also threatened to establish a permanent domination of British politics by the Whig-Liberal party. This possibility disappeared quite soon, but only because Conservatives recognised the importance of adopting liberal policies – a development in which Peel's 'Tamworth Manifesto' of 1834 played a crucial role.

After Disraeli became an MP his policies differed from Peel's in some respects, but he was initially a loyal follower of that statesman. If Peel had recognised the worth that Disraeli was sure he possessed and had given him office, Disraeli would probably have supported his changing policy throughout his ministry. Instead, he was frustrated by lack of office and took to attacking Peel and his policies, assuming a prominent role in his downfall. He was then confronted by the need to boost the fortunes of his truncated party so that it would gain in strength and obtain a majority which would give it an extended period in power. To this end it was necessary to adopt liberal policies. Some of these were direct continuations of Peel's approach, such as abandoning the defence of Protection and adopting social reforms. Others, notably taking up parliamentary reform, were innovations of his own.

Disraeli's policies were not invariably liberal, but nor were those of the Liberal party. He supported the restrictive Public Worship Regulation Act of 1874, but the Liberals had already passed the restrictive Ecclesiastical Titles Bill of 1851. He was a champion of imperialism, especially in the last few years of his life, and imperialism was not a liberal policy. But Liberals also defended the Empire, whether in Disraelian fashion or not, as Palmerston and Gladstone showed in their different ways. In this, as in other areas, the conflict between Disraeli and Gladstone was notably the product of their radically different personalities and styles rather than of any profound dichotomy over policy. In practically all spheres of their mutual engagement in policy – parliamentary reform, social reform, imperial and ecclesiastical matters – one can point to basic similarities outweighing more superficial differences.

Disraeli's policies were sometimes intended to complement the acts of Liberal Governments, rather than to duplicate them. At other times, however, he was in direct competition with the Liberals to pass a particular measure, as in the case of the Reform Acts of 1867–8. But whether he duplicated or complemented the Liberals, or lapsed from liberal policies altogether, Disraeli was generally an example of the limited liberalism which usually marked the policies of British Governments from the 1820s onwards. If he had attempted to go against this marked tendency in society and politics he would not have achieved his compelling object of rising to power.

· · ·

Disraeli was determined to vindicate the genius he believed was in him and to gain the utmost political power which the constitution of his country would allow. He realised his aim with interest, obtaining not only the premiership and a majority, but extending his influence beyond his 'isolationist' shores to negotiate a notable settlement at a celebrated international gathering. Whatever one thinks of the methods and policies he employed to attain his ends, his success was absolutely outstanding in rising so far from such relatively unpromising beginnings to reach such a pinnacle of power.

CHRONOLOGY

1804   Born, 21 December.

1817   Christened, 31 July.

1825   Failure of financial speculation; heavily in debt for forty years.
Failure of *The Representative*.

1826   First part of first published novel, *Vivian Grey* appears; arouses enmity of some influential Tories.
Continental journey.

1827–30   Suffers from nervous depression.

1830–1   Mediterranean tour.

1832   First candidature for Parliament, June.
First Reform Act passed, June.

1833–6   Affair with Lady Henrietta Sykes.

1834   Commences friendship with Lord Lyndhurst; thereafter drawn again into the Conservative party.

1835   Peel's 'Tamworth Manifesto' issued.
Clashes with Daniel O'Connell.
A Vindication of the English Constitution published, December.

1836   Elected to membership of Carlton Club.
Letters of Runnymede published.

1837   Accession of Queen Victoria, June.
Elected to Parliament, July.
Failure of maiden speech, 7 December.

1839   Marries Mary Anne Lewis, 28 August.

1841   Peel ministry formed; office refused to Disraeli.

1842–5 Leads the 'Young England' group.

1844   *Coningsby* published, May.
        Clashes with Government over factory hours and
            sugar duties.

1845   Clashes with Government over Maynooth Grant.
        Sybil published, May.

1846   Corn Law repeal crisis; repeatedly denounces
            Peel.
        Protectionist party formed.
        Defeat and resignation of Peel, 25 and 26 June.

1847   Returned for Buckinghamshire in general elec-
            tion, August.
        Speaks (on individual grounds) in favour of
            Jewish entry to House of Commons, Decem-
            ber.

1848   Death of Lord George Bentinck, September.
        Becomes owner of the Hughenden estate.

1849   Becomes virtual leader of Protectionists in Com-
            mons.
        Begins to want to abandon Protection.

1850   Death of Peel, 3 July.

1851   Ecclesiastical Titles Bill.
        Lord George Bentinck: a political biography published.

1852   Official leader of Protectionists in Commons.
        Chancellor of Exchequer for first time (after
            formation of Conservative Government), Feb-
            ruary.
        Protection abandoned.
        Advocates maintaining Maynooth Grant.
        Failure of Budget, December; resignation of
            Government.

1853   Begins to edit *The Press*; attacks Aberdeen Coal-
            ition and advocates Parliamentary Reform.

1854–6 Crimean War.

1855	Coalition resigns after defeat; attempt to form Conservative ministry abandoned; Palmerston becomes Prime Minister.
1857–8	Indian Mutiny.
1858	Conservative Government formed, February; Chancellor of the Exchequer for second time. India Bill passed.
1859	Introduces first Conservative Parliamentary Reform Bill in Commons, February; resignations from ministry. Reform Bill defeated, 31 March. Government resigns after defeat in Parliament, 11 June.
1859–65	Second Palmerston Government; Disraeli acts as Church establishment champion, particularly opposing anti-church rate bills.
1861	Death of Prince Consort, December; Disraeli's relations with Queen Victoria improve.
1862–3	Personal financial position greatly improves.
1864	Makes anti-Darwinian speech at Oxford, 25 November.
1865	Death of Palmerston, 18 October.
1866	Defeat of Russell's Government over Parliamentary Reform Bill, 18 June; Government resigns. Conservative ministry formed, June; Chancellor of the Exchequer for third time.
1867–8	Conservative Reform Bills and associated measures passed; Disraeli triumphs. Significant social reforms passed.
1868	Becomes Prime Minister, February. Abyssinian expedition succeeds. Bill to abolish compulsory church rates passed, with Government acquiescence. Defeated in general election and resigns, November.
1870	*Lothair* published, May.

1872 Conservative gathering at Burghley, January–February.
Speech at Free Trade Hall, Manchester, 3 April.
Speech at Crystal Palace, 24 June.
Death of his wife, December.

1873 Refuses invitation to form Government, March.
Speeches at Glasgow, November.

1874 Wins majority at last in general election, February; Prime Minister again.
Church of Scotland (Patronage) Act.
Ritualist controversy mounts; Public Worship Regulation Act.
Factory Act.

1875 Public Health Act.
Sale of Food and Drugs Act.
Conspiracy and Protection of Property Act.
Employers and Workmen Act.
Artisans Dwelling Act.
Balkan crisis begins, July.
British Government purchases forty-four per cent holding in Suez Canal, November.

1876 Merchant Shipping Act.
Education Act.
Royal Titles Act (Victoria becomes Empress of India).
Becomes Earl of Beaconsfield, 12 August.
Gladstone publishes *The Bulgarian Horrors and the Question of the East*, 6 September; and commences his agitation.

1877 –8 Russo –Turkish War.

1878 Resignations of Carnarvon and Derby from Cabinet.
Russian invading army stops short of Constantinople; British fleet sent there.
Treaty of San Stefano, 3 March.
Factory Act.
Congress of Berlin; fêted as international statesman.
Treaty of Berlin, 13 July.

1878–9   Economic depression grows.
Irish discontent; growth of demand for Home Rule.
Afghan and Zulu crises.

1880   Defeated in general election and resigns, April.
Endymion published, November.

1881   Dies, 19 April.

. . . .

BIBLIOGRAPHICAL ESSAY

(The place of publication is only given when it is other than London.)

. . .

BIOGRAPHIES

There has been a steady spate of biographies of Disraeli, varying greatly in length and depth, appreciation and condemnation, even some fictional ones having been contributed. The biographies began to appear well before his death (as early as 1852) and have extended to the present time. Some fifty of them have been published. The following is a selection, including the most important lives and all the recent ones.

Decidedly unfavourable to Disraeli is T. P. O'Connor, *Lord Beaconsfield: a biography* (W. Mullan and Son 1879). Much more sympathetic are T. E. Kebbel, *Life of Lord Beaconsfield* (W. H. Allen 1888; the Statesmen series); Sir William Fraser, *Disraeli and his Day* (Kegan Paul 1891); H. E. Gorst, *The Earl of Beaconsfield* (Blackie and Son 1900; the Victorian Era series); Walter Sichel, *Disraeli: a study in personality and ideas* (Methuen 1904); and J. A. Froude, *Life of the Earl of Beaconsfield* (J. M. Dent 1914, Everyman's Library; first edition 1890).

These and other early biographical contributions are but little foot-hills compared with the six lofty crests of W. F. Monypenny and G. E. Buckle, *The Life of Benjamin Disraeli, Earl of Beaconsfield* (six vols, John Murray 1910–20). Notably favourable to its subject, this massive compilation and study has been superseded in some respects by the findings of modern scholarship and the need for a more objective treatment. But the work remains valuable on account of its wide and detailed spread and the vast amount of correspondence which it presents.

After Monypenny and Buckle there was no further large biography for forty-six years, but the stream of fairly short ones continued, favourably in general to its subject: E. T. Raymond, *Disraeli: the alien patriot* (Hodder and Stoughton 1925); D. C. Somervell, *Disraeli and Gladstone: a duo-biographical sketch* (Jarrolds 1925); Sir Edward Clarke, *Benjamin Disraeli: the romance of a great career* (John Murray 1926); André Maurois, *Disraeli: a picture of the Victorian age*, translated by H. Miles (John Lane 1927); Wilfrid Meynell, *The Man Disraeli* (Hutchinson 1927); Sir Harold Beeley, *Disraeli* (Duckworth 1936; Great Lives, no. 65); Hesketh Pearson, *Dizzy: the life and nature of Benjamin Disraeli* (Methuen 1951); and Cecil Roth, *The Earl of Beaconsfield* (New York 1952). B. R. Jerman, *The Young Disraeli* (Princeton, NJ: University Press 1960) provides a detailed, scholarly and objective account of Disraeli's vicissitudes from his birth in 1804 to his entry to Parliament in 1837. Finally, there came another large, capacious life, resting considerably on the treasures in Monypenny and Buckle but also on a much wider range of sources and presenting a much more rounded view of its subject. This is Robert (later Lord) Blake, *Disraeli* (Eyre and Spottiswoode 1966). Blake has occasionally to be supplemented by more recent published findings, but his book remains the most scholarly combination of the political and personal approaches to Disraeli among the larger works on him.

Since Blake the lives have continued to flow, varying widely in length and purpose. Richard W. Davis, *Disraeli* (Hutchinson 1976), is a fairly brief study, very perceptive and searchingly critical. Sarah Bradford, *Disraeli* (Weidenfeld and Nicolson 1982), is a full, objective biography, surer on the personal than on the political side and providing new material on the former aspect. John Vincent, *Disraeli* (Oxford: University Press 1990; Past Masters series), is concerned primarily with Disraeli's thought as expressed through his writings, fictional and non-fictional, and suggests ways in which Disraeli may have influenced contemporary Conservatism. Also concerned partly with the relationship of

Disraeli to present-day Conservatism is John Walton, *Disraeli* (Routledge 1990; Lancaster Pamphlets); this makes suggestions over a wide range of Disraelian questions. The latest life, Stanley Weintraub's *Disraeli: a biography* (Hamish Hamilton 1993) is a long, pleasant, gossipy account, minutely detailed on the personal side but much less so on the political. Its most distinctive contribution is to air vague rumours that Disraeli fathered an illegitimate child or two, but virtually no evidence is cited to support them. An interesting recent article is Jane Ridley, 'The early career of Benjamin Disraeli: a fresh interpretation', *History Teaching Review Year Book*, vol. VII (1993), pp. 49–58.

The trend in producing comparative biographies of Gladstone and Disraeli, commenced by D. C. Somervell (see above), has been continued by Robert Blake, *Disraeli and Gladstone* (Cambridge: University Press 1969; The Leslie Stephen Lecture); J. Rooke, *Gladstone and Disraeli* (Wayland 1970; Documentary History series); and B. H. Abbott, *Gladstone and Disraeli* (Collins 1972; New Advanced History series).

. . .

SOURCES

As stated above, Monypenny and Buckle presents a great deal of Disraeli's correspondence, but the publication of editions of Disraeli's letters commenced well in advance of that work. Notably his brother Ralph Disraeli edited *Lord Beaconsfield's Letters, 1830–52* (John Murray 1887). After Monypenny and Buckle, the Marquess of Zetland edited *The Letters of Disraeli to Lady Bradford and Lady Chesterfield* (two vols, Ernest Benn 1929); and the Marchioness of Londonderry edited *Letters from Benjamin Disraeli to Frances Anne, Marchioness of Londonderry, 1837–61* (Macmillan 1938). More recently the monumental and comprehensive Toronto Project of editing and publishing Disraeli's letters (with abundant supplementary material) has commenced and progressed to 1847. In this invaluable and highly scholarly compilation J. A. W. Gunn, J. Matthews, D. M. Schurman and M. G. Wiebe have edited *Benjamin Disraeli: Letters*, vol. I (1815–34) and vol. II (1835–7) (Toronto: University of Toronto Press 1982); and Gunn, J. B. Conacher, Matthews and Mary S. Millar have edited *Benjamin Disraeli: Letters*, vol. III (1838–41) (University of Toronto Press 1987) and vol. IV (1842–7) (University of Toronto Press 1989). It is very much to be hoped that this edition will continue. It ranges far beyond the vast holdings of original correspondence in the Hughenden (Disraeli) Papers in the New Bodleian Library, Oxford, and the small collections in the British Library and the Fitzwilliam Museum, Cambridge.

Soon after Disraeli's death a collection of his speeches was edited by T. E. Kebbel, *Selected Speeches of the Late Earl of Beaconsfield* (two vols, Longmans, Green 1882). William Hutcheon edited *Whigs and Whiggism: political writings by Benjamin Disraeli* (John Murray 1913). Some intimate and useful information about Disraeli is given in John Vincent (ed.), *Disraeli, Derby and the Conservative Party: journals and memoirs of Edward Henry, Lord Stanley* (Hassocks: Harvester 1978). Disraeli's novels have been collectively published in the *Bradenham Edition of the Novels and Tales of Benjamin Disraeli* (twelve vols, Peter Davies 1926–7), and *Coningsby* and *Sybil* are currently available in Penguin Classics.

· · ·

ASPECTS

In addition to the treatment of Disraeli's attitudes, policies and activities in the biographies mentioned above, these matters are dealt with in the following books and articles.

Disraeli's emphasis on the inter-connections of Judaism and Christianity is displayed in his *Lord George Bentinck: a political biography* (Colburn 1851). His Jewishness is also treated in Sir Isaiah Berlin, 'Benjamin Disraeli, Karl Marx, and the search for identity', *Transactions of the Jewish Historical Society of England*, vol. XXII (1970), pp. 1–20; Michael Salbstein, *The Emancipation of the Jews in Britain: the question of the admission of the Jews to Parliament, 1828–60* (Associated University Presses 1982; The Littman Library of Jewish Civilization); and Paul Smith, 'Disraeli's Politics', *Transactions of the Royal Historical Society*, vol. XXXVII (1987), pp. 65–85.

Disraeli's Mediterranean travels are studied by Donald Sultana, *Benjamin Disraeli in Spain, Malta and Albania, 1830–2* (Tamesis 1976); and by Robert Blake, *Disraeli's Grand Tour:*

Benjamin Disraeli and the Holy Land, 1830–1 (Weidenfeld and Nicolson 1982).

The main study of Disraeli and social reform is the detailed, scholarly and wide-ranging account by Paul Smith, *Disraelian Conservatism and Social Reform* (Routledge 1967). An important re-interpretation is P. R. Ghosh, 'Style and substance in Disraelian social reform, c. 1860–80', in P. J. Waller (ed.), *Politics and Social Change in Modern Britain: essays presented to A. F. Thompson* (Hassocks: Harvester 1987), pp. 59–90.

The important subject of Disraeli and parliamentary reform has not received the thematic treatment which it deserves. But there is a detailed study of the 1859 Reform Bill in Angus Hawkins, *Parliament, Party and the Art of Politics in Britain, 1855–9* (Macmillan 1987). F. B. Smith, *The Making of the Second Reform Bill* (Cambridge: University Press 1966) gives not only a comprehensive account of that measure, but a detailed examination of previous bills. Other scholarly studies of the Second Reform Act are Maurice Cowling, *1867: Disraeli, Gladstone and Revolution – the passing of the Second Reform Bill* (Cambridge: University Press 1967; Studies in the History and Theory of Politics); and Gertrude Himmelfarb, 'The politics of democracy: the English Reform Act of 1867', in her *Victorian Minds* (Weidenfeld and Nicolson 1968), pp. 333–92.

Disraeli's overseas policy has received much attention. His contribution to the evolution of British imperialism is examined by C. C. Eldridge, *England's Mission: the imperial idea in the age of Gladstone and Disraeli* (Macmillan 1973); W. D. Macintyre, *The Imperial Frontier in the Tropics, 1865–75: a study of British colonial policy in West Africa, Malaya and the South Pacific in the age of Gladstone and Disraeli* (Macmillan 1967); Freda Harcourt, 'Disraeli's imperialism, 1866–8: a question of timing', *Historical Journal*, vol. XXIII (1980), pp. 87–109; Nini Rodgers, 'The Abyssinian expedition of 1867–8: Disraeli's imperialism or James Murray's war?', *Historical Journal*, vol. XXVII (1984), pp. 129–49; and P. J. Durrans, 'A two-edged sword: the Liberal attack on Disraelian imperialism', *Journal of Imperial and Commonwealth History*, vol. X (1981–2), pp. 262–84. A general survey of Disraeli's foreign policy is M. Swartz, *The Politics of British Foreign Policy in the Era of Disraeli and Gladstone* (Macmillan 1985). Disraeli's part in the Balkan question in the 1870s is examined in Richard Shannon, *Gladstone and the Bulgarian Agitation, 1876* (Thomas Nelson and Sons 1963, Nelson Studies in Modern History; second edition, Hassocks: Harvester 1975); R. Millman, *Britain and the Eastern Question, 1875–8* (Oxford: Clarendon Press 1979); and Richard Shannon, *The Age of Disraeli, 1868–81: the rise of Tory democracy* (Longman 1992; History of the Conservative Party, vol. II).

Disraeli's policies towards the Churches are examined in G. I. T. Machin, *Politics and the Churches in Great Britain, 1832 to 1868* (Oxford: Clarendon Press 1977), and *Politics and the Churches in Great Britain, 1869 to 1921* (Oxford: Clarendon Press 1987). In relation to the Public Worship Regulation Act of 1874, further detailed treatments are P. T. Marsh, *The Victorian Church in Decline: Archbishop Tait and the Church of England, 1868–82* (Routledge 1969), and J. Bentley, *Ritualism and Politics in Victorian Britain: the attempt to legislate for belief* (Oxford: University Press, 1978).

Theo Aronson, *Victoria and Disraeli: the making of a romantic partnership* (Cassell 1977) explores this particular idyll. The general liberalism of Disraeli's political approach after 1846 is emphasised through a study of his financial policy by P. R. Ghosh, 'Disraelian Conservatism: a financial approach', *English Historical Review*, vol. XCIX (1984), pp. 268–96. Parallels between Disraeli and an early eighteenth-century Tory are drawn in Richard Faber, *Beaconsfield and Bolingbroke* (Faber and Faber 1961).

Detailed critiques of Disraeli's novels are provided by Donald R. Schwarz, *Disraeli's Fiction* (Macmillan 1979), and Thom Braun, *Disraeli the Novelist* (Allen and Unwin 1981). An interesting edition of reviews of Disraeli's novels appearing over a 140-year period is by R. W. Stewart, *Disraeli's Novels Reviewed, 1826–1968* (Metuchen, NJ: The Scarecrow Press 1975).

. . .

BACKGROUND

Disraeli's career and policies can only be understood in relation to the economic, social and political developments of their day. The following works help to set his career in context. They are divided into more general and more specialised sections.

GENERAL

Asa Briggs, *The Age of Improvement* (Longmans, Green 1959); Donald Southgate, *The Passing of the Whigs, 1832–86* (Macmillan 1962); Harold Perkin, *The Origins of Modern English Society, 1780–1880* (Routledge and Kegan Paul 1969); J. H. Grainger, *Character and Style in English Politics* (Cambridge University Press 1969); Richard Shannon, *The Crisis of Imperialism, 1865–1915* (Hart-Davis, MacGibbon 1974); Robert M. Stewart, *The Foundation of the Conservative Party, 1830–67* (Longman 1978; History of the Conservative Party, vol. I); Norman Gash, *Aristocracy and People: Britain, 1815–65* (Edward Arnold 1979; The New History of England, vol. VIII); Donald Read, *England, 1868–1914* (Longman 1979); E. J. Evans, *The Forging of the Modern State, 1783–1870* (Longman 1983); Michael Bentley, *Politics without Democracy, 1815–1914: perception and preoccupation in British government* (Fontana 1984; History of England); Lord Blake, *The Conservative Party from Peel to Thatcher* (Methuen 1985); E. J. Feuchtwanger, *Democracy and Empire: Britain, 1865–1914* (Edward Arnold 1985; The New History of England, vol. IX); Bernard Porter, *Britain, Europe and the World, 1850–1986: delusions of grandeur* (Allen and Unwin 1987); Muriel Chamberlain, *'Pax Britannica'? British foreign policy, 1789–1914* (Longman 1988; Studies in Modern History series); Bruce Coleman, *Conservatism and the Conservative Party in nineteenth-century Britain* (Edward Arnold 1988); Robert M. Stewart, *Party and Politics, 1830–52* (Macmillan 1989; British History in Perspective series); Norman McCord, *British History, 1815–1906* (Oxford: University Press 1991; The Short Oxford History of the Modern World); Jonathan Parry, *The Rise and Fall of Liberal Government in Victorian Britain* (New Haven, Conn.: Yale University Press 1993).

SPECIALISED

Norman Gash, *Politics in the Age of Peel* (Longmans, Green 1953); W. D. Jones, *Lord Derby and Victorian Conservatism* (Oxford: Basil Blackwell 1956); H. J. Hanham, *Elections and Party Management: politics in the time of Disraeli and Gladstone*

(Longman 1959); Royden Harrison, *Before the Socialists: studies in labour and politics, 1861–81* (Routledge 1965; Studies in Political History); J. B. Conacher, *The Aberdeen Coalition, 1852–5* (Cambridge: University Press 1968); E. J. Feuchtwanger, *Disraeli, Democracy and the Tory Party: Conservative leadership and organisation after the Second Reform Act* (Oxford: Clarendon Press 1968); Paul Adelman, *Gladstone, Disraeli and Later Victorian Politics* (Longman 1970; Seminar Studies in History); Robert M. Stewart, *The Politics of Protection: Lord Derby and the Protectionist Party, 1841–52* (Cambridge: University Press 1971); Norman Gash, *Sir Robert Peel* (Longman 1972); J. T. Ward, 'Derby and Disraeli', in Donald Southgate (ed.), *The Conservative Leadership, 1832–1932* (Macmillan 1974); Angus Hawkins, *Parliament, Party and the Art of Politics in Britain, 1855–9* (Macmillan 1987); A. Macintyre, 'Lord George Bentinck and the Protectionists: a lost cause?', *Transactions of the Royal Historical Society*, fifth series, vol. XXXIX (1989), pp. 141–65; Richard Shannon, *The Age of Disraeli, 1868–81: the rise of Tory democracy* (Longman 1992; History of the Conservative Party, vol. II).

INDEX